Jesus on Health and Healing

David Muskett

O&U
Onwards & Upwards

Onwards and Upwards Publishers

4 The Old Smithy
London Road
Rockbeare
EX5 2EA
United Kingdom

www.onwardsandupwards.org

ISBN: 978-1-78815-979-1
Typeface: Sabon LT

About the Author

David is married with two grown up daughters, and lives in Hampshire where he is Methodist Superintendent Minister in the East Solent and Downs Circuit. Ordained in the Church of England in 1990, David has served churches in Bedfordshire and Surrey, moving to a Methodist Appointment in 2010 and transferring to the Methodist Church in 2013. He became Superintendent during the COVID-19 pandemic.

To contact the author, please write to:
davidjmuskett@gmail.com

Endorsements

Once again David has produced a book which takes key themes of Jesus' teaching in the Gospels and helps the reader explore them more fully. He weaves areas of the UK healthcare system, along with the challenges of a pandemic, into the accounts of health and healing that Jesus was involved in, and enables us to reflect on the clear message for our own lives today. David creates that bridge, which is vital when reading the Bible, to help make the link between Scripture and our everyday life. I also value the way that David draws our attention to the context in which the different Gospel accounts are set, so enabling us to see the bigger picture and the relevance of the teaching which impacts on many aspects of society. I found the book, in places, challenging me to re-think my role in God's Kingdom as well as that part of my ministry lived out in the life of the Church. I can imagine that, as well as being of value to the individual reader and explorer of faith, this book would provide a useful foundation for small Bible study groups.

Rev. Andrew de Ville
Methodist Minister
Chair of the Southampton District

In clear simple language, David in this book invites us to reflect deeply on Jesus the healer. Health and healing, or lack of them, concern people now as in Jesus' day. David's unfolding of what Jesus said and did then helps us to see what he is poised to do today.

Paul Johns
Methodist Preacher and formerly Director of the College of Preachers

Wherever David ministers, life, imagination and vision happen. I welcome and commend the latest of his writings. Be prepared to look at things differently.

Jonathan Frost
Bishop of Portsmouth

As with his previous books, David Muskett manages to combine a helpful analysis of the text, the context and cultural background of the chosen miracles in each short chapter. In *Jesus on Health and Healing* there is a wealth of suitably thematic material to help preachers searching for ways to illustrate and apply the miracles of Jesus.

Keith Field
Elder, Cranleigh Baptist Church

To Marian, Sarah and Zoë.

Contents

Foreword by Dr John Lockley

Here's an interesting question for you. What is the smallest muscle in the human body?

The answer is the *stapedius* – a muscle no more than 6 mm long inside each of our ears.

Six millimetres? Titchy! What does it do? Anything? And why is it needed? It's tiny! At that size it won't help you lift things more easily, will it? *So what does it do?*

Now here's a thought: does it make our hearing more sensitive? The answer is: not directly; in fact, quite the opposite. When the muscle is active it dampens down our acoustic sensitivity.

Curiouser and curiouser.

Have you worked out the answer yet? Then why not do what the psychologists and counsellors suggest: reframe it; in other words, look at the question from a different viewpoint.

And then it becomes obvious. Along with another tiny muscle (the *tensor tympani*) the stapedius muscle protects our delicate hearing mechanism from loud sounds. It does this by damping down excessive movements of the tiny bones in the ear which transfer sound vibrations from the eardrum to the place where the delicate auditory nerves do the actual sensing.

Now it all makes sense, doesn't it? These muscles are there to protect your hearing. It's the acoustic equivalent of screwing up your eyes when emerging from a darkened room into brilliant sunlight.

But there's a more general principle here, isn't there? It's often only when we see something in its entirety – but also in greater detail and in context – that we begin to understand in any depth its real purpose, and sense its full importance and its wider connections.

The same is true of the biblical accounts relating to Jesus, health and healing. The Bible contains many references to these events, often differing widely in their settings and their details. To understand the subject as a whole, we need to understand how all these events fit together; to be aware of the details; not to make assumptions; and to take note of surrounding influences, occurrences and pressures. These events took place two thousand years ago, in a far less scientific era; the accounts of them were recorded in a different language to ours (Greek), against the background of an existing religion (Judaism), in an occupied land (Judaea, as subjugated by the Romans), concerning a man who claimed to be the Son of God and who also appeared to be able to heal miraculously.

Nevertheless, as far as illness itself is concerned, Jesus wasn't a doctor: instead, He was a healer, with a particularly holistic approach. We won't learn much from the Bible about how He performed these miracles – because of course, that's what miracles are: supernatural. What we can learn, however, are the underlying teachings and principles connecting all these events: a network of details linking everything together but, even so, often in a pattern which we can't always perceive until we step back slightly in order to consider, and if necessary reframe, our understanding of the whole subject.

This is what Rev. David Muskett has done with his latest book, in a way which is specifically designed to help non-medical and medical readers alike understand how these disparate events are all part of a single consistent Christian approach to health and wholeness.

Dr John Lockley
Retired GP

Introduction

Jesus on Health and Healing seemed the obvious next title after *Jesus on Gardening* and *Jesus on Food*. Possibly it was more obvious than those! The COVID-19 pandemic made it all the more topical, though it also meant that opportunities to write became less frequent.

This volume, like its predecessors, is a collection of chapters which could be (and occasionally have been) used as sermons. They're written in that style, and reference is made in footnotes to some techniques which I use in my preaching. The book might also be used by individuals or groups looking for a thoughtful approach to Jesus' healing miracles without getting technically theological.

This volume is also like its predecessors in that it is not a medical textbook any more than the others were horticultural or culinary textbooks. It is worth saying a few things in introduction.

Our twenty-first century understanding of disease and illness of body and of mind is very different from that of the first century. This is particularly to be noted in the cases the Gospels present as possession. There would be differences of opinion among Christians, including among Christians with a medical knowledge, about the influence of the spiritual on human wellbeing of body and mind. Generally, most would say that almost all illness can be put down to pathological causes.

The other disease to comment on is leprosy. There are numerous accounts of Jesus 'healing lepers'. It should be said that the disease we now know as leprosy is not necessarily the same as the disease all these people suffered from who received healing from Jesus. Whatever the skin disease they actually suffered from in first century Palestine, when they encountered Jesus there were certain regulations. In this book, where I have assumed certain symptoms and effects for the individuals concerned, we cannot be certain of these.

These first-century texts are not about individual health problems. In spite of my chapter headings, Jesus is not addressing paralysis, ophthalmology, and so on. Jesus is primarily a healer rather than a medical practitioner or clinician. As such he looks at the whole person and not just the presenting physical or mental issue. That wholeness of approach also means that he sees the impact of the spiritual on each person as a part of their condition.

The twenty chapters are not an exhaustive collection of all the times when Jesus healed someone or had a conversation about a disease or condition. They do cover the main instances. Importantly, they show that whenever Jesus encountered someone with a disease, condition or disability, there are two factors at play in the encounter. There is Jesus' compassion for the individual and there is what the encounter and the outcome can show us about who Jesus was and is.

The second of these factors was the primary purpose of the writing of all four of the Gospel writers.

As with *Jesus on Gardening* where Jesus was never just talking about horticulture or agriculture, and as with *Jesus on Food* where Jesus' focus was never just on the context of eating and drinking, so with *Jesus on Health and Healing*. Jesus does tell us something about a first century Jewish view of disease and disability, but he is more focussed on the Kingdom of God and its coming in this world. Jesus healed not just so that someone would have a better quality of life; he healed people because being whole is the way they are intended to be and the way they will be in the Kingdom of the new creation.

David Muskett
Petersfield

1

Jesus on General Practice

Matthew 4:23-25

Jesus went throughout Galilee, teaching in their synagogues and proclaiming the good news of the kingdom and curing every disease and every sickness among the people. So his fame spread throughout all Syria, and they brought to him all the sick, those who were afflicted with various diseases and pains, demoniacs, epileptics, and paralytics, and he cured them. And great crowds followed him from Galilee, the Decapolis, Jerusalem, Judea, and from beyond the Jordan.

A GP sees many patients in a day with very varied symptoms ranging from coughs and colds to disintegrating joints, depression or symptoms of cancer, and many other possibilities. A GP has to deal with every disease and illness among the people.

Jesus seems to have gained a reputation as a general practitioner. *"Jesus went throughout Galilee ... healing every disease and illness among the people."*[1] His reputation was not confined to the area we think of as his home area of Galilee. *"News about him spread all over Syria..."*[2] Like a GP, he seems to have held surgery where *"people brought to him all who were ill with various diseases, those suffering severe pain, the demon possessed, those having seizures, and the paralysed"*[3]. His reputation was not just local or even regional but

---

[1]   Matthew 4:23
[2]   Matthew 4:24
[3]   Matthew 4:24

national: *"large crowds from Galilee, the Decapolis, Jerusalem, Judea and the region across the Jordan followed him "[4]*.

A similarity with the GP which is not apparent from Jesus' lifestyle is that he is able to take a holistic approach to each person who comes to him. GPs will have a medical history that might enable them to draw a conclusion about a presenting symptom without having to send a patient for tests. Where Jesus differs from the GP is that he also seems to be the specialist and doesn't have to refer anyone for treatment elsewhere.

Matthew's description certainly builds a sense of excitement and popularity. He shows that Jesus draws a crowd.

Let's pause for a moment to reflect on the nature of illness and disease before the development of modern medicine or even before what we might think of as primitive medicine. Many of the illnesses that are terminal today would not have been heard of as people didn't live long enough to contract them or they didn't have the means to establish what the disease was. People died of diseases that we now consider almost trivial in that they can be cleared up with a course of antibiotics. Alternatively they died of injuries that can now be treated relatively easily or are avoided through modern health and safety precautions and equipment.

It was clearly not Matthew's intention to promote Jesus to a modern health service as an alternative GP. Jesus' healings are only one aspect of Matthew's description of his ministry. Even within this description of Jesus as a general health and healing practitioner, there is a purpose beyond demonstrating his popularity and his power. There are clues in the first verse of our passage.

Jesus went throughout Galilee, teaching in their synagogues, proclaiming the good news of the kingdom, and healing...[5]

Matthew's mention of 'the kingdom' is one clue. Jesus' specialist subject was the Kingdom of God. Matthew usually calls it the Kingdom of Heaven to avoid offending Jewish readers' sensitivities about using the name of God. Occasionally, as here in Matthew 4:23, this is shortened simply to 'the kingdom'. Jesus seldom opened his mouth without talking about the Kingdom.

---

[4] Matthew 4:25
[5] Matthew 4:23

14

Other clues are in Matthew's summary of what else Jesus was doing. He was not simply a GP; he did more than practise as a health and healing worker; Jesus *"taught"* and *"proclaimed"* as well. He had a teaching and preaching ministry. To modern ears that might at first sound like a health professional in the congregation who also preaches from time to time.[6] But the way Matthew expresses it is clearly meant to indicate something much more integrated.

The practical outworking of the Kingdom that he proclaimed was the healing of *"every disease and illness"*. Jesus' teaching in their synagogues, in so far as we have examples of it, was about the fulfilment of the scriptures' prophecies of one who would come to bring the work of God's kingdom to earth. The vision of the Kingdom, as Jesus referred to it in his selection of a text from Isaiah,[7] is one of wholeness and justice, comfort and mercy for the poor, the broken-hearted and those who mourn.

These few verses are a summary at the beginning of Matthew's account of Jesus' ministry. They show us that his teaching and proclamation of the nearness of the Kingdom of Heaven go hand in hand with his general practice of the presence of the Kingdom.

Two other aspects of the context of this summary give us further clues to its interpretation.

Between verse 17 and verse 23 come verses 18-22![8] This is Matthew's account of Jesus calling his first disciples. The implication is that those he chose and called to follow him were to take part in this movement that preached a change of direction in people's lives because of the proximity of the Kingdom of Heaven.[9]

Those first four – Peter, Andrew, James and John – *"left their [fishing] nets and followed him"*[10]. And where they followed him was throughout Galilee where he was teaching, proclaiming and healing.

---

6   Examples might be a licensed lay minister, local preacher etc.
7   Luke 4:14-21; Isaiah 61:1-2;58:6
8   Many congregations where I preach would be used to me asking, "What comes between verse 17 and verse 23?" Some would be prompt with the answer, "Verses 18-22." Initially they might panic, thinking I expected them to be able to tell me the content of those verses! The device reminds us to look at the context of a passage.
9   Matthew 4:17 – 'repent' is a word with a sense of turning around.
10   Matthew 4:22

The other clue to the interpretation of verses 23-25 as a summary introduction to Jesus' ministry is in what follows.[11] Chapter 5 is clearly a new section but it follows directly on from chapter 4. Chapters 5-7 are known as the Sermon on the Mount and form the first of five major sections of teaching in Matthew's Gospel. Jesus taught his disciples about the nature of the Kingdom of Heaven that he proclaimed. As his teaching progresses it becomes clear that it is more than theoretical and more than a future event to look forward to. Jesus' teaching makes it clear that the nearness of the Kingdom is meant to be a practical reality in people's lives so that there is greater wholeness for individuals and for the community.

It is no wonder that Jesus seemed to be a GP when there was so much brokenness of body, mind and spirit around him that cried out to be made whole within the Kingdom of Heaven. Jesus' followers were and are called to be part of that healing, proclaiming and teaching.

There's a connection here with Matthew's account when Jesus sends his disciples to *"proclaim this message, 'The Kingdom of Heaven has come near.' Heal those who are ill..."*[12]

There would also seem to be a connection with the end of Matthew's Gospel where Jesus' disciples are sent to *"make disciples of all nations ... and teaching them to obey everything I have commanded you"*[13].

The implication is that Jesus' followers from those first four, including those who followed him during his earthly ministry and on through all those who have come after them for twenty centuries, are also called and sent to teach, proclaim and heal – to make whole.

That includes diseases and illnesses but should not be limited to the work of medical and health care professionals. Jesus' people are about wholeness of body, mind and spirit. We are to look for ways to promote the wholeness and healing of individuals and communities in practical ways. It involves personal wellbeing as well as the breaking down of barriers within communities and between different groups; it is personal, local, regional, national and international in its scope.

---

[11] Question: What comes after Matthew chapter 4? Answer: Matthew chapter 5. Matthew didn't put in the chapter divisions or headings.

[12] Matthew 10:7-8 (TNIV)

[13] Matthew 28:19-20

Jesus' general practice extends to his people practising general health, wholeness and wellbeing at every level. We are all GPs in the Kingdom of Heaven, and we pray for the Kingdom to come on earth in the same way as it is in heaven.

2

Jesus on Possession (1)

Mark 1:21-29

They went to Capernaum; and when the sabbath came, he entered the synagogue and taught. They were astounded at his teaching, for he taught them as one having authority, and not as the scribes. Just then there was in their synagogue a man with an unclean spirit, and he cried out, 'What have you to do with us, Jesus of Nazareth? Have you come to destroy us? I know who you are, the Holy One of God.' But Jesus rebuked him, saying, 'Be silent, and come out of him!' And the unclean spirit, throwing him into convulsions and crying with a loud voice, came out of him. They were all amazed, and they kept on asking one another, 'What is this? A new teaching – with authority! He commands even the unclean spirits, and they obey him.' At once his fame began to spread throughout the surrounding region of Galilee.

As soon as they left the synagogue, they entered the house of Simon and Andrew, with James and John.

Whether people speak with authority and what authority lies behind the pronouncements of people in the public gaze is a very current issue. Politicians all around the world can be seen to assert an opinion without backing it up with facts or authoritative research. If asserted often enough and forcefully enough, an opinion becomes a 'fact'. And yet the only authority behind it is the voice of the one who spoke it in the first place. Sometimes that politician is a popular, elected leader whom people may think ought to be aware of the circumstances surrounding what they say. But still, the only authority is that person's own opinion.

By contrast, experts are often derided if the results of their research conflict with the opinions people want to believe. Expert opinions, based on the authority of research in political, economic and scientific fields, are brushed away as 'scaremongering', 'project fear' or anti-democratic, or placed on an equal footing with that of someone who has a vested interest in an opposite opinion.

Jesus taught with an authority that was noticeably different from the authority of the priests, the scribes and the Pharisees. Jesus didn't list his bibliography of Rabbis' writings or put in footnotes for the scriptural references for what he taught. Jesus simply asserted the nature of the Kingdom of God. His authority came not from his reading and learning, but from his intimate relationship with God. Jesus simply proclaimed the proximity of the Kingdom. He knew it from the inside and came to show in a new way how God is King.

At this point it sounds as though I'm promoting the assertive, opinionated politician who lacks facts and research over the experts who base their conclusions on thorough research. All parallels only work to a certain extent. The point is that it is easy to see how Jesus got a popular following. He taught with personal authority about the nature of God's Kingdom as a place of wholeness and healing, for binding up the broken-hearted, freeing the captives and oppressed, and giving sight to the blind and comfort to the oppressed. This was clearly and explicitly taken from Isaiah 61, but Jesus' authoritative, personal slant was that it was fulfilled in him.

If this vision of the Kingdom of God was being made real in their present time, it is no wonder people went along to hear him and be part of the movement that seemed to be gaining momentum from Jesus' base in Capernaum on the northern shores of Galilee.

Both Mark and Luke give accounts of this event in the synagogue at Capernaum at the beginning of Jesus' ministry and make it clear that there is more to it than that. Before we put Jesus in the same bracket as a clever politician who can whip up a crowd by asserting some opinions that have little basis in facts, we need to look a little closer at the context. When it comes to interpretation, context is always the most important tool.

What we have is not just an account of some authoritative teaching. There is a practical outworking of his teaching that makes a real difference for an individual in exactly the way he has been talking about.

In the synagogue was a man possessed by a demon: an evil or unclean spirit.

Modern medicine and psychological and psychiatric knowledge have found many other ways to describe the symptoms that are used of those who are called 'possessed' in the biblical narratives. Any disease that involved loss of control like epilepsy, delirium, convulsions, hysteria, nervous disorders or mental derangement would have been said to be caused by a demon.

This is not a medical diagnosis, but a religious or a spiritual one. To make this diagnosis is to say that illness and disease make the world and the people in it not the way God wants them to be. The fallen nature of the world extends into every aspect of human life and it is only the superior power of God that can ultimately rescue us from that.

Mark has set out from the start that Jesus' purpose was to proclaim the Kingdom of God. Luke's first mention of the Kingdom of God is in this passage. In this way he makes clear the practical implications of the coming of the Kingdom. When God comes near to bring his reign to bear upon human life, there is an authority beyond that of the experts. This authority is also far beyond the assertions of the opinionated. The newly authoritative teaching of Jesus shows how God's ways work in practice. Jesus' previously unseen authority is seen to triumph over all that works to divide, oppress, restrict and disintegrate.

In his narrative, Mark doesn't give as much of the content of Jesus' teaching as Matthew and Luke do. This indicates different approaches to knowing God's ways when it comes to practical, day-to-day situations.

The Jewish way in the time of Jesus, based upon the practice of the scribes and Pharisees, was to consult the Scriptures and the tradition. In Christian terms, that would be to see what the Bible has to say and what various authorised and respected preachers and teachers have had to say over the centuries. Jesus is presented in continuity with this line, especially by Matthew and Luke. He takes the scriptural and traditional teaching and takes it a step further. *"You have heard it said ... but I say to you..."[14]*

The other approach appeals less to the organised rational, logical, fact-based mind. In biblical terms, it is characterised by St Paul's saying *"we have the mind of Christ"*. By reflection on the Scriptures, by prayer and meditation, by inhabiting the ways of the Kingdom as preached by Jesus and his followers, we come to a view for our own time. Jesus is also seen in continuity with this line, especially by Mark. We're not told the content of his teaching, but its authority is clear from the response of the demons and the people who saw and heard what happened.

What Mark establishes at the beginning of his narrative of Jesus' ministry is that Jesus spoke and acted with the present authority of God's Kingdom, so that their longing to be freed from the evils of the world could be fulfilled. The evils that possess many of us in so many different ways seek to destroy and divide and cause chaos and confusion. Jesus meets that possession with the calm authority of God's ways of life and wholeness.

As with much of all of the Gospels, in this instance in a synagogue in Capernaum, early in his account, Mark points us towards what was ultimately and eternally fulfilled as Jesus hung on the cross at the end of his earthly life. At that point, as here, the earthly and spiritual powers of evil cry out and recognise what's happening and know that they can no longer hold on to that which they have possessed. Jesus comes, and in his life, his ministry of word and actions, and in his death and resurrection, he frees us from possession by all that destroys and divides in favour of all that gives life – eternally.

---

[14] e.g. Matthew 5:21 and five other instances in the same chapter

3

Jesus on Leprosy (1)

Mark 1:40-45

A leper came to him begging him, and kneeling he said to him, 'If you choose, you can make me clean.' Moved with pity, Jesus stretched out his hand and touched him, and said to him, 'I do choose. Be made clean!' Immediately the leprosy left him, and he was made clean. After sternly warning him he sent him away at once, saying to him, 'See that you say nothing to anyone; but go, show yourself to the priest, and offer for your cleansing what Moses commanded, as a testimony to them.' But he went out and began to proclaim it freely, and to spread the word, so that Jesus could no longer go into a town openly, but stayed out in the country; and people came to him from every quarter.

Our skin is the largest organ in our bodies and something we often take for granted – until something goes wrong or affects it in some way.

You are very likely to have experienced some damage to your skin as a result of falling over as a child and grazing your knee. You may have cut yourself while cooking or doing DIY; you may have pricked your finger with a needle. All damage the skin to some extent, and the result can be painful, messy and unsightly, depending on the severity and the part of your skin that you puncture.

But those are not skin diseases.

You may have had a disease or a condition that has come out in a rash or affected the skin in some way. Measles and chicken pox are obvious childhood diseases that show signs on the skin. Leprosy is also a disease that affects the skin. The word translated 'leprosy' was used in New Testament times for various diseases that affected the skin. Whether the disease this man had who approached Jesus was actually leprosy or something else is immaterial, as he was being treated as one who had leprosy.

It meant he lived isolated from other people because the disease was treated as extremely contagious. He was also regarded as 'unclean'; his disease had practical implications around his spiritual life as well as his social and economic life. Illness and disability could be *healed;* leprosy had to be *cleansed.* The Hebrew scriptures have the example of Naaman the Syrian who was cleansed from his leprosy by Elisha. The rabbis knew this was difficult and said that cleansing leprosy was as hard as raising the dead.

Perhaps that's why Mark puts this incident in his narrative at this point. At this point we've read about healing people with diseases; we've seen that Jesus relieved people of possession by evil spirits; we've heard about him gathering disciples, teaching and praying. An introductory section that culminates in something as hard as raising the dead sets the scene for what Jesus' whole life, ministry, death and resurrection are to be all about.

A GP has a knowledge of a wide range of diseases and conditions and may often know the patient over a long period of time. This shows us that Jesus has all that and more: he is a specialist in every aspect of health and healing.

This episode is charged with emotion. The man with leprosy *"begged Jesus on his knees"*[15]. It conveys an intensity way beyond the words he used. Jesus' emotional response is comparable. The translation varies from *"Jesus was indignant"*[16] to Jesus being *"moved with compassion"*[17]. Either way, what is intended is that we understand the intensity of Jesus' emotional response.

Is he indignant or angry because the man's question implied that he might *not* be willing? Or is he angry because someone is in this condition and needs to be cleansed in order to take his place in the world alongside others? Or is he simply filled with pity for this individual and wants to extend the compassion to him in that practical way?

---

[15] Mark 1:40
[16] TNIV
[17] NKJV

No doubt many who are involved in health care or have chosen a caring role do so out of compassion for the various ways in which human beings suffer through disease, isolation and disability. Jesus demonstrates that wholeness of life for this individual was something that is at the heart of God's purposes.

Jesus' instruction to him to show himself to the priest and offer the sacrifices as required by the law showed that he wanted to be seen to be operating within the law. Jesus also told him not to tell anyone. That may simply mean that Jesus didn't want to precipitate a crisis by being misinterpreted. It perhaps indicates that his purpose is about more than the restoration of health and wellbeing to as many people as he could come across in the time that was available. Maybe when Jesus addresses matters of health and healing, that's not all that's on his mind. Maybe the wholeness of individuals is also about a wider wholeness of being that is part of God's purpose.

It can be said of some people that they can keep anything except a secret. It is said of some governments that they leak like a sieve. And yet there are some who were involved in secret war work who took that extremely seriously and never told another living soul about what they had been doing even after many decades.

This man was unable to contain himself. He couldn't help but tell everyone what had happened. He spread the news that he had come across Jesus, who was able to do something as hard as raising the dead. There's an emotionally intense response in that as well. He was unable to keep it secret and simply do what was required. He couldn't help telling people what Jesus had done for him.

The law required sacrifices as testimony,[18] but a much more powerful testimony was his own account to his friends and family and apparently anyone he met who would listen.

You may not have been healed of leprosy – or any other disease affecting the skin – but maybe Jesus has enabled you to mix with others, or engage in an activity you never thought you could. Maybe it is by being part of a church that you have found acceptance and inclusion that has overcome the prejudice or exclusion that you found elsewhere. Maybe being one of Jesus' followers and going along with others has given you a sense of purpose or overcome an isolation.

---

[18] Mark 1:44

Whatever it is, don't be content with 'what the law requires'. Talk freely, spread the news. In the words of a song we sang when our children were small, *"Stop, and let me tell you what the Lord has done for me."*

This man had a dramatic, emotionally charged story to tell. What's your story? It doesn't have to be as dramatic or emotionally intense, but if there's something in it that explains why you are who you are, it's a story worth telling.

4

Jesus on Healing at a Distance

Matthew 8:5-13

When he entered Capernaum, a centurion came to him, appealing to him and saying, 'Lord, my servant is lying at home paralysed, in terrible distress.' And he said to him, 'I will come and cure him.' The centurion answered, 'Lord, I am not worthy to have you come under my roof; but only speak the word, and my servant will be healed. For I also am a man under authority, with soldiers under me; and I say to one, "Go", and he goes, and to another, "Come", and he comes, and to my slave, "Do this", and the slave does it.' When Jesus heard him, he was amazed and said to those who followed him, 'Truly I tell you, in no one in Israel have I found such faith. I tell you, many will come from east and west and will eat with Abraham and Isaac and Jacob in the kingdom of heaven, while the heirs of the kingdom will be thrown into the outer darkness, where there will be weeping and gnashing of teeth.' And to the centurion Jesus said, 'Go; let it be done for you according to your faith.' And the servant was healed in that hour.

During the COVID pandemic there was a marked acceleration in the trend for doctors to do consultations over the phone. It saves time and can be much more convenient for a patient who might find it difficult to get to a surgery. The doctor can give advice about the likely severity of the complaint based on a description of symptoms in much the same way as they can when a patient is in the surgery. They can make a diagnosis and issue prescriptions, and drugs may be delivered or collected from a pharmacy with no direct contact between doctor and patient.

Doctors know there are elements of a consultation that are missing when it is not face-to-face, but are generally keen to save precious time in the surgery. For many years, doctors have been reluctant to do home visits unless absolutely necessary, for similar reasons.

It would display great faith in a doctor if a patient in a telephone consultation said that they felt a bit unwell and they were sure that was all the information the doctor needed to prescribe the right medication to make them better. This episode with Jesus and the centurion's servant's illness is even further removed than that.

It would be surprising if a doctor offered to visit a patient but was told that wouldn't be necessary because a word spoken into the air by the doctor sitting in the surgery would be enough.

Jesus has expressed confidence in his ability to heal the servant based only on the symptom that he is paralysed and suffering terribly. But he offers to go and do a home visit. Although it would give him the opportunity to find out if there was anything that might have caused the paralysis and if there was any history of physical impairment, Jesus didn't need that. The offer to go to the centurion's home is to be seen in the context of the centurion's faith.

Matthew and Luke both have an account of this story and there's another that only differs slightly in John's Gospel. In all accounts the centurion is commended for his faith.

It is worth making sure we understand what is meant by faith. Often when we hear about 'people of faith' or 'faith groups', it is a way of describing those who have a belief in some spiritual realm to which all or some people might go after death. Equally it describes those who believe in a spiritual being beyond our physical experience.

'Faith' is a word closely related to 'trust' and 'reliance'. It is much less intellectual and much more practical than usually interpreted. The writer to the Hebrews gave us a definition: *"Faith is being sure of what you hope for, certain of what you do not see."*[19] He goes on to give examples of those who lived by faith in that they were sure of their hope for 'a better place'. Those heroes of faith lived as though God

---

[19] Hebrews 11:1

could be relied upon even when their actual circumstances didn't look very promising.

In this episode the centurion is not commended for his understanding of Jesus' medical abilities. This centurion bypasses any sense of Jesus' medical knowledge and homes in on his authority. Jesus has no certificate and his name doesn't appear on any list of qualified medical practitioners; he wears no uniform and carries no identification badge; and yet the centurion recognises his authority in the matter of his servant's paralysis.

He's a man who knows about authority. He exercises authority over those in the company of soldiers that he commands and over his servants in his household. He also knows what it is to be under authority and exercise the authority he has because it was given to him from someone of superior rank to him. It looks as though he sees something similar in Jesus when it comes to a person who is unwell.

He says to Jesus, *"I am a man under authority, with soldiers under me. I tell this one, 'Go,' and he goes; and that one, 'Come,' and he comes. I say to my servant, 'Do this,' and he does it."*[20] The implication is that he says to Jesus, "You can say to this disease, 'Go!' and it goes; to that paralysis, 'Be cured!' and it is cured."

The centurion calls Jesus *"Lord"* which is probably simply a mark of respect, like calling the doctor 'sir'. But the Gospel writers use it to remind readers of Jesus' status as Lord, in the sense of the one who has been given all authority in heaven and earth.[21]

Jesus uses the centurion's response of faith to comment on the nature of faith in relation to the Kingdom in which he has been given all authority. It is clearly part of Jesus' purpose that the Kingdom would be open to Gentiles as well as Jews, even if the mission to Gentiles was not to begin in earnest until after his death and resurrection.

By recognising Jesus' authority over his servant's paralysis, the centurion lived as if the rule of Jesus' Kingdom was already in place, even though he couldn't yet see it in any other practical way.

---

20 Matthew 8:9 (TNIV)
21 Matthew 28:18

5

Jesus on Fever and General Practice

Luke 4:38-44

After leaving the synagogue he entered Simon's house. Now Simon's mother-in-law was suffering from a high fever, and they asked him about her. Then he stood over her and rebuked the fever, and it left her. Immediately she got up and began to serve them.

As the sun was setting, all those who had any who were sick with various kinds of diseases brought them to him; and he laid his hands on each of them and cured them. Demons also came out of many, shouting, 'You are the Son of God!' But he rebuked them and would not allow them to speak, because they knew that he was the Messiah.

At daybreak he departed and went into a deserted place. And the crowds were looking for him; and when they reached him, they wanted to prevent him from leaving them. But he said to them, 'I must proclaim the good news of the kingdom of God to the other cities also; for I was sent for this purpose.' So he continued proclaiming the message in the synagogues of Judea.

It's likely that a doctor can never quite feel off duty. Doctors in church and other social groups always run the risk of being asked about their friends' medical conditions and even the illnesses of members of friends' families.

In this episode Jesus had been at synagogue, and when faced with a man diagnosed as demon-possessed, he cast the demon out with a command. We've seen in chapter 2 that this was a practical demonstration of the authority that came to him directly from God. The Jews believed that God is eternally King, but in so many ways the world didn't and doesn't look like it. It is as though others have usurped God's power. Demon possession may look very like many different aspects of mental illness but it is a spiritual diagnosis. Jesus' coming was the beginning of the reestablishment of God's reign, which would be fulfilled in his ministry, death and resurrection.

In the synagogue he couldn't be off duty, because the health and wholeness of those he met was as important a part of his message as the teaching he gave about freedom and sight and good news for the poor, the blind and the oppressed. He might have thought that after synagogue he would get a break over lunch with his friend Peter. But, like a GP, he can't quite relax and forget his role. Peter's mother-in-law has a fever.

Jesus' treatment of her indicates that when he addresses health issues, it is not only the health of the patient that is being considered. We read Luke's account of what happened but, as with other aspects of Jesus' life, we also need to ask what it's all about.[22]

Casting out a demon from a man possessed is a way of seeing that Jesus was addressing the reassertion of God's kingly authority. It looks from this episode with Peter's mother-in-law as though all illness could be seen in a similar way. Those who are laid low by illness are not as they should be. The fever meant that Peter's mother-in-law was unable to take her place in the family and the community; she was in bed.

These two healings took place while he was supposed to be 'off duty'. The Sabbath was a time for rest from work. The locals seemed to have more respect for that than Jesus, who didn't tell the demon-possessed man or Peter's mother-in-law to come back at sunset. But when the sun went down and the Sabbath was over, it is as though the surgery opened and the waiting room was full of people with various

---

[22] Readers of *Jesus on Gardening* and *Jesus on Food* will already be familiar with the question, "What's that all about, then?" as a way of getting behind the events to see what the biblical writers are telling us about God and what God is doing.

kinds of illness. Once again, we're told what happened. But, what's it all about then?

Perhaps there's a clue in how Luke describes the way Jesus healed. In the synagogue Jesus had simply commanded the demon to *"come out of him"*[23]. With Peter's mother-in-law he had *"rebuked the fever"*[24]. With the queue in the surgery waiting room he *"laid hands on each one"*[25] and as demons came out of patients *"he rebuked them"*[26].

It is a very simple method. Just as Jesus' teaching in the synagogue doesn't refer to previous authoritative sources and learning, so his medical practice is not dependent on medical textbooks or getting the right drugs to prescribe. There are no magic formulae, no higher power, no 'hocus pocus' in words and actions appealing to any power beyond his own. He makes simple commands and lays hands on people.

As so often, the invaluable tool for interpreting an event in a biblical narrative is the context in which it is set. The healing of Peter's mother-in-law with her fever followed by Jesus in the 'GP surgery' come after Jesus has been at synagogue.[27] While there, he healed the demon-possessed man. Earlier in the chapter – still part of the context – Jesus was also in a synagogue where he preached on a carefully chosen passage from Isaiah.

Chapter 4 is the start of Jesus' ministry, following on from Luke's genealogy which traces Jesus' supposed descent from Joseph back to Adam, the son of God.[28] The way each section begins in chapter 4 gives a sense of progression from one event to the next, even if they were actually separated by several days or a week. Luke didn't include chapter or verse divisions; we're meant to read it as a single account. So, the healings in the synagogue and home in Capernaum and in a public place follow on from the teaching in the synagogue in Nazareth.

---

[23] Luke 4:35
[24] Luke 4:39
[25] Luke 4:40
[26] Luke 4:41
[27] See note 8 on p.15.
[28] Luke 3:23-38

Jesus doesn't need to appeal to any higher power or authority because he is the *"Son of God"*[29], anointed by the Spirit of the Lord[30] to release the oppressed, give sight to the blind and loose the chains of the prisoners. This covers political and health matters, but is by no means confined to them. The other part of the context is what comes after verse 41 (verses 42-44).

Here we understand what Luke is telling us through his narrative about Jesus' purpose in God's wider scheme. Jesus needs to keep moving – partly for the benefit of the town and the surrounding population. Becoming a place where crowds gathered day after day seeking healing would create a reputation and an unsustainable situation. He hadn't come to start a local alternative to the health centre, and he had come for a wider purpose than being known as a healer.

The main reason he had to keep moving was to go where people were, to bring the message that God was becoming King in a new way. This is Luke's first mention of *"the Kingdom of God"*. Jesus spells it out when they try to stop him moving on: *"I must proclaim the good news of the kingdom of God to the other towns also, because that is why I was sent."*[31]

What Luke describes is crowds gathering for a popular message of liberation and personal wholeness all coming from an authority that is unsourced but undeniable. This can be seen as threatening. It is not much longer in Luke's narrative before we find opposition following Jesus around. Where Jesus' people today have a similar message of a higher authority than the local political leadership and a personal wholeness that is not dependent on drugs and therapies, they can still be seen as threatening the established authorities.

How would it be if Jesus' people now spoke about how life should be and the importance and priority of making it so for the poor, the disabled, the oppressed and disadvantaged? Jesus' message and his healings link together. On a very practical, obvious and political note, surely it means that if a country has any means at its disposal, the right thing to do is provide proper resources to health and social care, those

---

[29] Luke 3:38
[30] Luke 4:18
[31] Luke 4:43

32

who support the weak, disadvantaged and marginalised? That is surely still the good news of the kingdom of God.

The only difference is that because of Jesus' life, ministry, death and resurrection, God is already King.

6

Jesus on Possession (2)

Mark 5:1-20

They came to the other side of the lake, to the country of the Gerasenes. And when he had stepped out of the boat, immediately a man out of the tombs with an unclean spirit met him. He lived among the tombs; and no one could restrain him any more, even with a chain; for he had often been restrained with shackles and chains, but the chains he wrenched apart, and the shackles he broke in pieces; and no one had the strength to subdue him. Night and day among the tombs and on the mountains he was always howling and bruising himself with stones. When he saw Jesus from a distance, he ran and bowed down before him; and he shouted at the top of his voice, 'What have you to do with me, Jesus, Son of the Most High God? I adjure you by God, do not torment me.' For he had said to him, 'Come out of the man, you unclean spirit!' Then Jesus asked him, 'What is your name?' He replied, 'My name is Legion; for we are many.' He begged him earnestly not to send them out of the country. Now there on the hillside a great herd of swine was feeding; and the unclean spirits begged him, 'Send us into the swine; let us enter them.' So he gave them permission. And the unclean spirits came out and entered the swine; and the herd, numbering about two thousand, rushed down the steep bank into the lake, and were drowned in the lake.

The swineherds ran off and told it in the city and in the country. Then people came to see what it was that had happened. They came to Jesus and saw the demoniac sitting there, clothed and in his right mind, the very man who had had the legion; and they were afraid. Those who had seen what had happened to the demoniac and to the swine reported it. Then they began to beg Jesus to leave their neighbourhood. As he was getting into the boat, the man who had been possessed by demons begged him that he might be with him. But Jesus refused, and said to him, 'Go home to your friends, and tell them how much the Lord has done for you, and what mercy he has shown you.' And he went away and began to proclaim in the Decapolis how much Jesus had done for him; and everyone was amazed.

As usual, what happened is reasonably easy to work out from this encounter between Jesus and a man clearly suffering from severe mental illness, not unreasonably described as demon possession. The man saw Jesus coming and went to meet him. After an exchange that gave some idea of his affliction, he was healed, and in the process a large herd of pigs was destroyed. Ultimately the man was persuaded to be reintegrated into his community while Jesus moved on.

So far, so straightforward.

Asking "What's that all about, then?" of this passage reminds us of other aspects of context as a tool for interpretation. In this case we need to select the four aspects of context that are geographical, socio-religious, historical and political.

Geographically this takes place somewhere on the eastern side of the Sea of Galilee among the Decapolis – the Ten Towns. There is some uncertainty about exactly which of the towns was nearest, which is reflected in varying translations. The key point is that it was not Jewish territory. Some socio-religious context shows us that the locals were keeping pigs; Jews wouldn't be doing that.

Another piece of the socio-religious context is that, to a Jew, the whole setting is filled with uncleanness. Pigs and those who kept them were unclean according to Jewish law. The dead and graveyards were also unclean, and contact with them would make a person also unclean.

It is intriguing but unproductive to ask why Jesus went there in the first place. We can never reach an answer to that. It is possible to speculate with hindsight that Jesus knew in advance what would occur and he wanted to demonstrate that his mission was to include the outcast, the unclean and Gentiles. Alternatively, he may simply have needed a break, put out to sea and that was where the wind took them. Ultimately, such speculation is unproductive. I shall simply put it down, along with a growing list of such questions, as something I shall ask someone when I get to heaven!

Historically, it is always worth reminding ourselves that any event recorded in the New Testament took place in the first century AD, and events in the Gospels are around the end of the third decade or beginning of the fourth. Politically, that means the whole area is under Roman domination. The Roman army was everywhere, keeping an uneasy peace. People would be allowed to live if they did as they were told and kept on the right side of the occupying forces. Local collaborating politicians would do OK; tax collectors and prostitutes might do well. The Roman Legions were The Enemy. Many Jews dreamed of a Saviour – Messiah – who would drive the Romans into the Mediterranean Sea.

The sea is another part of the socio-religious context. Jews, to whom Mark's Gospel was originally addressed and among whom it's content would have circulated in oral form before it was written down, saw the sea as the source of chaos. It was, therefore, fitting perhaps, that the cause of chaos and disintegration ended up in the sea.

Already a parallel between the bigger picture of the wider historical-political context and the detail of one individual begins to emerge.

Perhaps this individual has become obsessed to the point of possession by all things Roman – especially all things violently and negatively Roman. It is not unknown for superhuman strength and hysterical behaviour to be associated with such obsessive illnesses. Finding a psychological parallel doesn't necessarily remove any possibility of forces outside our power or understanding which might get a grip on people's minds, especially under such stressful and dangerous historical-political circumstances. It looks as though the man who came out from the tombs to meet Jesus was so obsessed by the alien forces around him that had taken over his country, that he had become possessed by an internal legion of invaders who had taken over his personality and crushed his humanity. It left him naked, isolated, violent and self-destructive.

So, at a very simple level, the answer is clear. What this is all about is that the individual circumstances represent the nation. The Kingdom of God is Jesus' favourite subject and what he came to establish, so what he did also indicates aspects of the Kingdom. God's Kingdom means healing and the restoration of justice to Israel and the world, so the unclean and oppressive must be banished into the sea.

The man's legion of demons stands for the Roman Legions.

But it's not quite as simple as that.

We've seen a bigger picture than this individual and his obsessive-possessive disorder. But surely Mark is pointing us to something more than a first century political point. Surely there is something spiritual going on as well.

What we may have noticed but haven't pointed out yet is the parallel between this individual's situation, cure and rehabilitation and what Mark will tell us about Jesus and the climax of Jesus' story as Mark tells it.

Jesus ends up tortured, naked, isolated and dying among the tombs. He takes on all that the world has dealt to this individual. That is how healing takes place in God's eternal, spiritual scheme of things through Jesus.

If we dig that little bit deeper for the other parallels, this story tells us of the spiritual battle as well as the personal and the political battles. In our interpretation of the Bible, it is important not to find we can't see the wood for the trees. Don't miss that bigger, eternal perspective.

But conversely, we must take in the detail of the trees. The big story is told through an incident involving an individual. It has a clear focus on detail that needs to be carried into the detail of our own lives twenty centuries later. Jesus met a man with deep human need, afflicted by the chaos of being possessed by an internal version of external forces that had become his obsession. Jesus met his need and healed that distress.

One of the points that this story is all about, in terms of Jesus on health, is that wherever humans are in pain and distress, Jesus' mercy, healing, comfort and compassion need to be expressed and applied. Jesus' big story is that he identified with those in pain and distress, possessed by powers outside their control or understanding. On the cross he took the full evil force of The Enemy and let the others go free. For Jesus' people today, the interpretation is plain: Jesus calls us to bring his message of mercy, healing, comfort and compassion to every community because it is in every community that people are in pain and distress.

Again, the parallel is there in the man from the tombs. He wanted to go with Jesus, stay with Jesus, know what he felt to be the safety and security of being close to Jesus all the time. But Jesus wouldn't let him. In that sense we have an advantage in being part of the church and having received the gift of the Holy Spirit; Jesus' promise that he would be with us always to the very end of the age[32] can be fulfilled along with the charge he gave to the man from the tombs: *"Go home to your own people and tell them how much the Lord has done for you, and how he has had mercy on you."*[33]

This man's new life depended on Jesus in a different way; perhaps he found that the Spirit gave him strength and inspiration among his family and friends in his home and community. What is clear is that before Paul coined the phrase or claimed the title, this man was an apostle to the Gentiles. All those of us who have known Jesus' healing and restoration, and know him to embody the Kingdom of God, have the same charge: *"Go home to your own people and tell them how much the Lord has done for you, and how he has had mercy on you."*[34]

---

[32] Matthew 28:20
[33] Mark 5:19
[34] Ibid.

7

Jesus on Paralysis

Matthew 9:1-8

And after getting into a boat he crossed the water and came to his own town.

And just then some people were carrying a paralysed man lying on a bed. When Jesus saw their faith, he said to the paralytic, 'Take heart, son; your sins are forgiven.' Then some of the scribes said to themselves, 'This man is blaspheming.' But Jesus, perceiving their thoughts, said, 'Why do you think evil in your hearts? For which is easier, to say, "Your sins are forgiven", or to say, "Stand up and walk"? But so that you may know that the Son of Man has authority on earth to forgive sins' – he then said to the paralytic –'Stand up, take your bed and go to your home.' And he stood up and went to his home. When the crowds saw it, they were filled with awe, and they glorified God, who had given such authority to human beings.

We need to reclaim the neutrality of the word 'authority'. 'Authority' and 'the authorities' tend to have negative connotations. We think of endless, unnecessary red tape and regulations created by anonymous bureaucrats apparently with the sole purpose of making life awkward. Alternatively, we think of oppressive regimes and violent enforcement of laws whose sole purpose is to preserve the power of those who have it and assert that power over anyone who disagrees.

Authority, seen more neutrally, is about what gives someone the right to exercise their power. In the case of oppressive regimes, power is exercised because they have it – there is an army to back up the power with force. In a democracy, power is exercised because of the outcome of an election. The source of such authority is the ballot box.

A doctor's authority comes from being on the Medical Register, for which they need training, experience, testing and qualifications. So-called alternative therapists are also regulated so that those who consult them with various diseases and conditions know that the person they consult speaks with some authority on their subject.

Before we come to the authority to forgive sins, which is what this encounter between Jesus and a man who was paralysed seems to be about, we need to remind ourselves what sin is all about. A good-enough definition is 'the human tendency to make a mess of things'.

That might be expanded upon by saying that because it is a human tendency, no one is exempt from it. In technical terms, what Paul wrote to the Romans is true: *"All have sinned..."*[35] It is worth noting that the rest of that verse adds to our definition: *"All have sinned and fall short of the glory of God."*[36] If there were no tendency to make a mess of things, there would be no mess and all would live as God intended, in the image of God and therefore in perfect wholeness of being and community.

But there is sin; there is a human tendency to make a mess of things. So often – day by day, hour by hour – each of us does and says things that offend our neighbours, upset our family, make life difficult for others, assert ourselves at the expense of someone else, even if we don't overtly attack anyone or explicitly call them by unwarranted and untrue labels. Much of that stems from thoughts and attitudes within us that put ourselves first, with anyone else a distant second.

Having established what sin is, I want to recognise that much of the time most people are not like that and there are many acts of kindness that clearly put others first. There are many who love their neighbours by seeking to meet the needs of those around them before their own. All of that is good and the goodness of human beings is to be celebrated.

But it is not a profit and loss account. It is not about whether the goodness outweighs the badness. A prominent serial abuser from history is said to have commented that when it came to the divine judgement, he would be OK because of all the charitable causes he had

---

[35] Romans 3:23
[36] Ibid.

supported. The comment of one minister was that he didn't think it worked like that. He was right; it doesn't work like that. In God's economy the tendency to make a mess of things is not rectified by an effort to do some good things. In God's economy sin is wiped away by forgiveness.

The encounter between Jesus and a man who was paralysed directly addresses the forgiveness issue and where the authority to forgive comes from. In Matthew's account, which is much shorter than the same story in Mark and Luke, this is clearly the main point. Mark and Luke give more detail about friends who bring the man on his bed and the difficulties they overcome to get him to Jesus. This relates more to faith, which is another important theme and we'll come to it in a moment.

Something that leaps at us from all the accounts is the connection between the man's paralysis and his need for forgiveness. In the ancient world the perceived connection between sin and disease or disability was much stronger than it is today. Often the link was seen as causal: sin led to disease or disability. We'll see this in chapter 16 when Jesus was asked about a blind man, *"Who sinned, this man or his parents, that he was born blind?"*[37]

Of course, we are not told the cause of the man's paralysis. He may have had an accident at work that left him unable to move his legs. He may have contracted a disease such as Multiple Sclerosis that had gradually left him more and more immobile. The link with sin and forgiveness may suggest a psychological and symbolic understanding. Perhaps he had done something, or lived a life of which he was deeply ashamed. He felt trapped by whatever it was; he knew he was guilty and saw no way to escape from it. Gradually the sense of guilt ate away at him; perhaps he developed a sense that whatever he did would go wrong, or be wrong in someone else's view. Eventually this sense of guilt and being a 'wrong person' stopped him doing anything at all; he stopped moving and he stopped getting out of bed.

There is one more step before we come back to what this passage says about authority. We now come to the matter of faith. Jesus saw the faith of those who brought the man on his bed.[38] We must assume the man had agreed to be taken, so Jesus also saw the faith of the man

---

[37] John 9:2
[38] Matthew 9:2

himself. Faith, as we've seen before, is *"being sure of what you hope for, certain of what you do not see"[39]*. What, then, did those friends and the man on the bed hope for that they could not yet see?

The story gives us two possibilities. They hoped for healing so that he would be able to get up and walk. They – or at least he – hoped for forgiveness that would free him from his overwhelming sense of guilt. Perhaps it was not so explicit. Maybe they just hoped that Jesus would be able to do something about it. But to hope for something that seems very unlikely is just optimism. Jesus saw their faith, not a desperate optimism.

Because he saw their faith, Jesus the healer knew that he could address the root cause and the symptoms would quickly disappear. There is no miracle drug for this man's paralysis; there is no regime of treatment, no availability of steroid injections. Jesus' authority for treating this man's paralysis, as for his treatment of fevers, possession and other diseases, comes directly from God. It is worth remembering that what Jesus came for, and addressed on almost every occasion we hear from him, was the Kingdom of God. So, Jesus goes straight to the heart of the matter and uses his authority to pronounce the forgiveness of this man's sins.

We can see that this is the main point for Matthew in telling the story. He has edited the version he found in Mark's account so as to leave only what is necessary around the discussion with the teachers of the law. The authority to forgive sins was clear at the time and was focused in those who had the relevant qualifications under the law and were registered to pronounce that forgiveness. Obtaining forgiveness involved the sacrificial system at the Temple and the ministry of priests with the right background and training. The reasoning was that only God could forgive sins, and individuals had to do all the right things in order to know that he did grant that forgiveness to them in their particular instance.

Jesus clearly acted outside that system in telling the man on the mat that his sins were forgiven when he interrupted a preaching moment in a house in Capernaum. Matthew tells us what happened with minimal detail but with a certain clue to what it is really all about and his purpose in telling it. The clue is in what Jesus says about his authority.

---

[39] Hebrews 11:1

"...I want you to know that the Son of Man has authority on earth to forgive sins."[40]

When Jesus refers to himself in the third person as *"Son of Man"*, the reference is always to Daniel 7 where the *"son of man"* will be enthroned in judgement over all the forces of evil.[41] By adopting that title for himself, Jesus is saying that his authority comes directly from God and he is already acting to declare that sin is defeated and new life can begin.

That's how it works for this individual. But, as always, there's a bigger picture that Matthew is showing, of which this is a detail. The Israel of Jesus' day was paralysed by the oppression of Rome and hoped for the coming of a Messiah to sit in judgement over all that restricted them and give them the new life of God's people.

This episode may be seen as symbolic of that bigger picture but it really speaks to something on an even larger canvas. Jesus' coming as Son of Man addresses the deeper and darker evils of sin that are so symbolically referred to in Daniel's visions. If the result of this man's sins is his paralysis, the result of sin on the wider landscape is death.[42] Perhaps paralysis is symbolic of death, which is the ultimate inability to move.

The final clue to this story being also about Jesus' ultimate purpose is in the words Jesus addressed to the man on the mat and Matthew's description of what he did. *"[Jesus] said to the paralysed man 'Get up, take your mat and go home.' Then the paralysed man got up and went home."*[43] The word for *"Get up"* is 'arise', and connects in our minds with Jesus' resurrection. When sin is dealt with, resurrection – new life – cannot be far behind.

What applied to an individual crippled by guilt in first century Palestine applies similarly to anyone conscious of their tendency to make a mess of things today. Jesus' life, ministry, death and resurrection show us that the Son of Man has authority on earth to forgive sins and God has extended that authority to his representatives today as he did then.

---

[40] Matthew 9:6
[41] Daniel 7:13-14
[42] Romans 6:23
[43] Matthew 9:6-7, emphasis added

That leaves two challenges.

1. If you're conscious of your tendency to make a mess of things, come to Jesus, the Son of Man, who extends forgiveness to you so that you too can 'arise' and live a new life in God's ways as a citizen of his Kingdom. Perhaps find some friends to help you.

2. Your faith might help to carry a friend to Jesus. If someone you know is paralysed by a sense of guilt, or just conscious that they're 'not good enough', help to carry them to the Son of Man, tell them that God does forgive, he does wipe the slate clean. Give them the hope, and help them arise to live a new life in God's ways as a citizen of his Kingdom.

8

Jesus on Disability (1)

Matthew 9:1-8

Again he entered the synagogue, and a man was there who had a withered hand. They watched him to see whether he would cure him on the sabbath, so that they might accuse him. And he said to the man who had the withered hand, 'Come forward.' Then he said to them, 'Is it lawful to do good or to do harm on the sabbath, to save life or to kill?' But they were silent. He looked around at them with anger; he was grieved at their hardness of heart and said to the man, 'Stretch out your hand.' He stretched it out, and his hand was restored. The Pharisees went out and immediately conspired with the Herodians against him, how to destroy him.

This account of a dispute with the Pharisees is clearly about Sabbath observance rather than disability. As with many of the occasions when Jesus addresses some aspect of health and healing, that is not the whole of what the story is about. It looks as though the Pharisees and other synagogue officials knew that this *"man with a shrivelled hand"* would be there. It is possible that he was invited along or placed in a prominent position in the front row, so as to set a trap to catch Jesus out.

It may also be significant that he had a *"shrivelled hand"* or some kind of disability, rather than an acute illness or demon possession, as in previous examples, that may have posed an immediate danger to himself or to others. It leads us to believe that he suffered from a condition that was ongoing and probably had been with him for some time, if not since birth. It may have been the result of an accident at work.

The point is that he could have gone to find Jesus (or any other person with a healing reputation) on the following day, rather than lead Jesus to break Sabbath regulations by healing on the Sabbath.

It's not a particularly subtle trap, and Jesus sees straight through it. And he doesn't dodge the issue. Rather abruptly, he gets the man to stand up in front of everyone and uses him as the example for a challenging question about Sabbath observance.

"Which is lawful on the Sabbath: to do good or to do evil, to save life or to kill?"

The implication of the question is that not to heal would be contrary to God's ways. To heal would obviously be to do good. No one is suggesting that to have ignored his condition would have killed him, but it certainly wouldn't have enhanced his life or given him back any of the freedoms that had been curtailed by his disability.

The silence of the Pharisees indicates that the answer to Jesus' question is self-evident. They also didn't know how to express their resentment regarding his implication that their stance was tantamount to doing evil or killing, which were clearly not lawful on any day of the week. Perhaps they realised that when he asked about killing, it was not a reference to the man with the shrivelled hand. He was about to do good and to give life to the disabled man. They were planning to do evil in plotting to kill Jesus.

There are a number of conclusions we could draw from this, not all of them necessarily compatible.

Firstly, it looks as though Jesus drives a coach and horses through Sabbath regulations, indicating that the law should only be treated as a guideline and not enforced, even if doing so would only *postpone* a good action.

Secondly, we might apply it to attempts to Keep Sunday Special. When Sunday trading regulations were significantly relaxed and there were more and more leisure opportunities on Sundays, many church people felt that Sabbath regulations were threatened. Certainly, more people had to work on Sundays than had previously been the case. Some took this passage to mean that this was the right thing and Jesus didn't approve of the traditional Sabbath anyway.

What the Sabbath regulations of Old and New Testaments and Church tradition don't recognise is the two-day weekend of Saturday and Sunday or 'days off' on weekdays that still constitute Sabbath for those who have them.

More significantly in the context of this passage is that Jesus is referring to 'work' that is life-enhancing for others. It seems to be rather stretching a point to call it work when Jesus simply told him to stand in front of everyone and stretch out his hand. He gave him no exercises, no prosthetic surgery and no drugs. In reaching out to this man and drawing attention to him as he saw through the duplicity of the Pharisees, Jesus simply acknowledged his humanity and his needs and ensured he could live a life of wholeness.

In the context of leisure activities and shopping, it might be possible to say that giving people more of that opportunity is life-enhancing rather than life-restricting. There is a danger of falling into a similar trap to the Pharisees though. While encouraging these life-enhancing activities, the qualification should also be made that those who are required to work to make that possible should also have time off – Sabbath – to pursue their own life-enhancing activities.

A third conclusion might come from Jesus' reaction of anger and distress at the silence that indicated their stubborn hearts. In Mark's account this is the end of a series of incidents that have caused controversy and opposition. Jesus sees hypocrisy in their determination to adhere to the letter of the law. They have an ideological stance that won't be swayed by scenarios that are self-evidently right and good and life-giving but contrary to their position.

The hypocrisy of the Pharisees' position is underlined by their decision to plot with the Herodians. The Herodians were supporters of Herod Antipas, whom the Pharisees usually thought of as a dangerous traitor to Judaism and the Jewish nation. Jesus was a fellow rabbi. It's just that he seemed to have some rather liberal views on the law. It seemed better to the Pharisees to plot with an opposition party against a fellow Jew whose interpretation of the coming Kingdom of God was rather wider than theirs.

Finally, it is worth pointing out that this controversy arose over the Sabbath – not simply the law in general. Sabbath had many resonances with Jewish history, starting from God's rest on the seventh day of creation and its place in the law given at the Exodus. Sabbath had become an emblem of Jewishness in their present, and a symbol of the great future of freedom and rest when God would liberate them from pagan oppression.

Perhaps unsurprisingly this early in Jesus' ministry, the Pharisees did not appreciate that in Jesus the freedom of the new creation and true redemption had already arrived. This wasn't just a challenge to a legalistic interpretation of the Sabbath. Jesus was the embodiment of the new order of true freedom and rest.

For us today, it is worth asking if we have appreciated that even now, or do we still get so bogged down in our rules and regulations that we fail to take hold of God's healing and restoration that enhances rather than diminishes life?

In practical terms we might also be challenged about the realisation of Sabbath in our own times. Jesus did not come to abolish the law and the prophets but to fulfil them.[44] Surely that includes the life-enhancing aspects of a rhythm of work and rest. How do we speak and work for that against the economic forces that make wealth-creation the ultimate goal and ride rough-shod over the health and wellbeing of the people on which it is dependent?

---

[44] Matthew 5:17

9

Jesus on Disability (2)

John 5:1-15

After this there was a festival of the Jews, and Jesus went up to Jerusalem.

Now in Jerusalem by the Sheep Gate there is a pool, called in Hebrew Beth-zatha, which has five porticoes. In these lay many invalids – blind, lame, and paralysed. One man was there who had been ill for thirty-eight years. When Jesus saw him lying there and knew that he had been there a long time, he said to him, 'Do you want to be made well?' The sick man answered him, 'Sir, I have no one to put me into the pool when the water is stirred up; and while I am making my way, someone else steps down ahead of me.' Jesus said to him, 'Stand up, take your mat and walk.' At once the man was made well, and he took up his mat and began to walk.

Now that day was a sabbath. So the Jews said to the man who had been cured, 'It is the sabbath; it is not lawful for you to carry your mat.' But he answered them, 'The man who made me well said to me, "Take up your mat and walk."' They asked him, 'Who is the man who said to you, "Take it up and walk"?' Now the man who had been healed did not know who it was, for Jesus had disappeared in the crowd that was there. Later Jesus found him in the temple and said to him, 'See, you have been made well! Do not sin any more, so that nothing worse happens to you.' The man went away and told the Jews that it was Jesus who had made him well.

Have you ever felt that someone seems to operate in a different world? Or have you been accused of coming from a different planet? It's where there's a disjunction between one person's assumptions about life and the way things operate in 'the real world'. It may be that a person's background culture is different in some ways from the culture in which they live. Most of the time you don't notice, but occasionally there are customs that stand out as different from what you expected.

There are two ways in which this is pertinent as we come to an episode from John's Gospel. Most importantly, it is more noticeable in the way John records events that Jesus functions from a background and culture that is from the Kingdom of God and the new creation, and this comes up against the culture of the world as we know it.

Secondly, but importantly as we seek to interpret John's Gospel, John also seems to operate under different cultural norms in his writing. Even more than other New Testament writers, it is important to note where detail might be revealing symbolism and making connections. We can read what John says happened, but even more than elsewhere we need to be aware of what he's telling us it's really all about, hidden in or revealed by the details of the story.

John has given us the clue that this is the case by describing as 'signs' the first two of Jesus' miracles that he recounts. Signs point us to something beyond themselves. By this stage of his narrative, John expects us to be able to count for ourselves. In a sense, which number we've got to is not important, but knowing that there are eight in total, with Jesus' own resurrection as the last, is significant.

Jesus comes to Jerusalem for a festival. He's at the heart of the Jewish religious system. The exact name for the pool in question is hard to pin down from various translations, though its location seems to have been identified by archaeologists. Because the name is variously given, it may translate as House of Olives or House of Mercy.

John describes the surroundings in terms of five covered colonnades.[45] If we're looking for symbolism, we might notice that at the heart of Jewish religion, providing shelter and the origins of the religion, were the five books of the Law of Moses. It is in the 'waters' of the law that the Jews were to find their wholeness.

---

[45] John 5:2

The presence of many, variously disabled people has resonances with Jesus' account of the Great Banquet where the *"blind, the lame, the paralysed"*[46] are welcomed. Jesus homes in on one of them: a man who is paralysed and has been by the pool seeking its healing for thirty-eight years. We might ask, now we're getting used to seeing symbolism everywhere, why we're told how long he's been there. Whether it is an accurate record of the time he waited or just a number to make a point doesn't detract from the point that it makes. Thirty-eight years was the time the people of Israel wandered and waited in the wilderness after the giving of the law before they entered the Promised Land.[47]

Perhaps this man represents his people?

Jesus asks him, *"Do you want to get well?"*[48] The implication of the question is that coming to the pool has become his way of life and he is content to continue in that routine. Remembering the symbolism, we can read that John is suggesting that the Jewish people have become content with the ritual and routine of the law and are not really looking for what will make them whole – just as perhaps by the time the Israelites had been in the wilderness for thirty-eight years, they had become used to the wandering wilderness lifestyle.

If we also remember that the Bible continues to speak words of encouragement and challenge to us, we may also ask ourselves whether our religious customs have become a comfortable routine. Have we stopped looking for the life-affirming, healing power that is at its heart? Have we become so focused on the journey that we've forgotten that there is a Promised Land, a new creation, the Kingdom of God as a destination?

Back at the pool, the man gives a typical self-justifying and self-pitying account of why he has been there so long. In doing so he fails to answer Jesus' question. *"Sir, I have no one to help me into the pool when the water is stirred. While I am trying to get in, someone else goes down ahead of me."*[49]

It seems an odd and unjust system that the patients at the head of the queue are the ones who are least disabled or the ones who have a greater support network to help them. Perhaps there's a message here

---

[46] John 5:3
[47] Deuteronomy 2:14
[48] John 5:6
[49] John 5:7

for the organisation of health services. Maybe there should be within the system a way of ensuring that it is those with greatest need and least additional support who are treated first? It seems that for this man it was not a thirty-eight-year waiting list, just that every time his name got near the top, someone else came into the waiting room not with greater need but greater means of getting noticed, and their papers went on top of the pile of those to be seen.

Again, back at the pool, Jesus does as we have seen him do on previous occasions. His style is similar to his approach in the synagogue in Capernaum with the man with the shrivelled hand.[50] His words are almost the same as with the paralysed man brought to him by friends.[51]

"Get up! Pick up your mat and walk."[52]

It is a simple command. It is just words. It is in no sense work – though the doing of it was. *"At once the man was cured; he picked up his mat and walked. The day on which this took place was a Sabbath."*[53] This was a Sabbath and regulations were clear that carrying your mat on the Sabbath was counted as work.

At no point in the narrative has faith been mentioned. Even at this point the word is not used, but it is the carrying out of the command to *"Get up! Pick up your mat and walk"* that constitutes faith. He must have seen something in Jesus that gave him the confidence to do something that he may have longed for but had become unable to do. Before Jesus came, he couldn't see how this was possible. With Jesus in front of him, challenging his routine contentment with a broken life, his hope for wholeness was rekindled. He became sure of what he hoped for, certain of what he could not see, to the extent that he did as he was told.[54]

As we see more of the possibilities of the new creation that Jesus brings through his life, ministry, death and resurrection, maybe we can have our hope rekindled and our confidence grown to say and show that there is a way to live that is the life of the Kingdom of God, rather

---

50 Mark 3:1-6; see chapter 8
51 Matthew 9:6; see chapter 7
52 John 5:8
53 John 5:9
54 Hebrews 11:1

than the routine brokenness of the world with which we become comfortable.

Until the second half of verse 9, John has just given his account of the healing. It is as though he wants to address some of its implications separately. As far as Jesus addressing matters of health goes, we have already seen that there is a bigger picture of which an individual disabled person is one detail. John goes on to fill in more of the background.

The debate about the place of Sabbath and Sabbath regulations continues but this is where John helps us see that Jesus is functioning out of a different set of cultural assumptions. He's not in the Jewish religious world view sheltering under the five colonnades of the books of the Law of Moses. He's coming from the world view of the new creation and his signs point to its coming. The final sign will be the dawning of the new creation: the eighth sign on the first day of the (new) week and therefore the eighth day – one day beyond the Sabbath.

Jesus' work is to do the will of the one who sent him, and that means losing no opportunity to point towards the Kingdom and the way life should be in all its fullness.[55]

We may have noticed that in contrast to the healing of the paralytic who was brought by his friends,[56] the issue of sin is not raised until Jesus seeks him out later. *"Stop sinning or something worse may happen to you"*[57] can be variously interpreted.

Some say that it is about final judgement, and that case would not be hard to make. Some say that it indicates that his paralysis was as a result of his sin. We've seen in our assessment of the paralytic in Matthew that this could be the case but the link here is barely implied, not really made. It would be easier to say that illness, disease or disability can be caused by sin. That is no doubt the case but it is not universally so. There are many illnesses that are not caused by sin and many sinners who are healthy.

When he says, *"Stop sinning or something worse may happen to you,"* Jesus is telling him not to take his new wholeness for granted. He is well, whole, healthy – something that could not be said of him while he lay paralysed on his mat. The wholeness that Jesus gives is

---

[55] John 10:10
[56] Matthew 9:1-8
[57] John 5:14

not simply physical. Unless he understands that he is well in every sense, he will revert to being a broken part of a broken world rather than a sign of the new world to come.

Let's live as signs of the world to come and seek to mend the brokenness of our world where the poor, the marginalised, the sick, the disabled and the oppressed go to the back of the queue. Let's meet them and be those who bring them to the source of ultimate healing in the one who transforms and supersedes the waters of the old order.

10

Jesus on Gynaecology and Childhood Illness

Luke 8:40-56

Now when Jesus returned, the crowd welcomed him, for they were all waiting for him. Just then there came a man named Jairus, a leader of the synagogue. He fell at Jesus' feet and begged him to come to his house, for he had an only daughter, about twelve years old, who was dying.

As he went, the crowds pressed in on him. Now there was a woman who had been suffering from haemorrhages for twelve years; and though she had spent all she had on physicians, no one could cure her. She came up behind him and touched the fringe of his clothes, and immediately her haemorrhage stopped. Then Jesus asked, 'Who touched me?' When all denied it, Peter said, 'Master, the crowds surround you and press in on you.' But Jesus said, 'Someone touched me; for I noticed that power had gone out from me.' When the woman saw that she could not remain hidden, she came trembling; and falling down before him, she declared in the presence of all the people why she had touched him, and how she had been immediately healed. He said to her, 'Daughter, your faith has made you well; go in peace.' While he was still speaking, someone came from the leader's house to say, 'Your daughter is dead; do not trouble the teacher any longer.' When Jesus heard this, he replied, 'Do not fear. Only believe, and she will be saved.' When he came to the house, he did not allow anyone to enter with him, except Peter, John, and James, and the child's father and mother. They were all weeping and wailing for her; but he said, 'Do not weep; for she is not dead but sleeping.' And they laughed at him, knowing that she was dead. But he took her by the hand and called out, 'Child, get up!' Her spirit returned, and she got up at once. Then he directed them to give her something to eat. Her parents were astounded; but he ordered them to tell no one what had happened.

I don't remember a pandemic like the COVID pandemic, but every few years or so there is a disease that threatens to spread throughout the world and some precautions are necessary. You may remember SARS and others like it before that.

The numbers of NHS staff and medical professionals around the world who have died, including the first doctor to raise awareness of the disease, does make me wonder why doctors are not permanently ill. Surely, they are more in danger of infection through contact with so many sick people?

St Paul refers to Luke as *"the beloved doctor"*[58], so maybe he had more insight into sickness and healing than others of his time. We don't know what kind of illness Jairus's daughter had, but the story within her account is of a woman subject to continual menstruation. Luke is not particularly pointing out the medical risks of treating the sick. He is pointing out something similar within the religious tradition.

First century Palestine was several hundred years before the development of soap as we know it. As far as we know, the slogan 'Hands, Face, Space' had also not yet been invented. But at least two of the elements of it might have been familiar.

The Jews, like many cultures, especially in hot climates, had developed purity laws for a very practical purpose. Some of them involved washing – but not with soap and water for twenty seconds. It is what we might describe as quarantine or isolation. Being unwell meant a need to maintain a distance from others so as not to pass anything on. This exclusion also extended to the demands of religious ritual because they were significant times when groups of people came together. In an age before radio and television, let alone Zoom, an

---

[58] Colossians 4:14

individual who was sick was unable to engage in worship or offer the expected sacrifices.

This exclusion from such gatherings also extended to those who had contact with anyone who was sick or who had died because they might have caught the disease as well. It was like the track and trace system requiring you to isolate if you'd been in contact with COVID or if you were returning from somewhere on the Red List.

To modern eyes it is unreasonable to include a condition of continuous debilitating menstruation, which probably had a psychological origin, in the same bracket as infectious diseases, but in religious terms it had the effect of making her permanently 'unclean'[59].

Something else that seems strange to modern eyes used to a modern health care system is that two such different cases should be in the waiting room for the same consultant. The woman has apparently already consulted several physicians and has a condition that today would require the attention of a gynaecologist. Jairus' daughter has a mystery illness which may have been as simple to us as measles or a similar childhood ailment that would now be treated with antibiotics or prevented by immunisation as an infant.

They seem two very different cases but they both come to Jesus, and there are other factors that link them, making it interesting as well as appropriate to read and think of them together. The obvious connection is that Jairus' daughter was twelve years old and the woman had been suffering from her condition also for twelve years. It might be possible to speculate on any significance in that coincidence, especially given Luke's previous inclusion of a story none of the other evangelists tell, about the twelve-year-old Jesus in the Temple.[60] Twelve is, of course, the number of tribes of Israel and the number of disciples, but why should a sick child and a woman with a gynaecological condition also feature the number twelve? Unless it is some kind of code to show that women, children and the sick and marginalised can also be included in the new people of God as his Kingdom is established.

The main spiritual connection is 'faith'. Immediately after she is discovered as the person who touched him, causing power to go out of him, Jesus tells the woman that her faith has healed her. Overhearing

---

[59] Leviticus 15:19-30
[60] Luke 2:41-50

the message that Jairus' daughter has died, Jesus tells him to 'have faith'. The faith that Jairus was to have must surely have been helped by seeing Jesus declare that power had gone out of him even before he knew who had been healed. Witnessing the effect of her faith when she simply touched Jesus must have encouraged Jairus to wonder what might be possible if Jesus would come and touch his daughter.

It is the common theme of touch that brings us back to the issue of social and religious exclusion. Jesus is doubly polluted. It is because of the uncleanness issue that the woman came to touch him furtively. But Jesus deliberately touched the body of the dead girl. Whether deliberately or not, Jesus broke through an established taboo, with instant and astonishing results.

There are two interesting conclusions to be drawn from Jesus' reaction to the woman who touched him in the crowd. He knew that power had gone out of him. It appears that every cure cost him something in spiritual energy. We should remember that although it is what they are trained and paid for, our medical professionals are also vulnerable human beings. It also costs them in physical and emotional energy as they treat patients throughout the day and night.

Secondly, Jesus found it necessary to embarrass the woman with publicity rather than let her slip away into comfortable obscurity. She may then have suffered a relapse brought on by guilt at having broken the laws of uncleanness. Or she may have enjoyed a permanent cure and lived a more connected life. However, by being made to go public with her testimony, she was able to receive Jesus' blessing for her actions and see the cure as a gateway to life under the grace and fatherhood of God. Perhaps we need to be challenged to be more public about what Jesus does for us and how Jesus welcomes us when we come to him seeking his grace and help?

So, in so far as Jesus addresses either gynaecological conditions or fatal childhood illnesses, it is not to say that they require particular specialists but that in the eternal scheme of God's Kingdom they do not require the exclusion that had become the law and custom, even if for ostensibly logical reasons. Clearly this is an example of Luke's care about, and interest in, stories about women, which he highlights more than the other Gospel writers. But it is also about Jesus himself. All the Gospel writers have the same primary purpose: to show who Jesus is and what he has come to achieve.

In these incidents Jesus shares the pollution of sickness and death and turns them into the wholeness and hope of life by the power of his love. Jesus' love shines though in this account, as it will through Luke's account of Jesus' arrest, suffering and death when, as an innocent person, he takes on the suffering and death of those who are guilty. This raising to life as he speaks to the girl saying, *"My child, get up,"[61]* points towards his own raising to life through the power of the love of God.[62]

What it tells us about Jesus both then and now is that it is his presence, his touch that makes the difference. Whatever the problems or suffering we face, the presence of Jesus getting involved, risking and being infected by the dirt and grime of this world, is what we need. The good news that the Gospel writers promise is that this is what God does in and through Jesus and continues to do in and through his Spirit working in and through his people today. As he did with a woman in the crowd who would have preferred to remain anonymous; as he did with the president of the local council of elders at the synagogue and his daughter, wife and friends; so he still does with us in our confusion, our fear and the mess we make of things.

Jesus welcomes our fearful, nervous reaching out to touch with words of peace.[63] He responds to our hesitant and fearful requests as he did then, and as he has for centuries since, with the command most often repeated in the Bible: *"Do not be afraid."[64]*

---

[61] Luke 8:54
[62] Luke 24:7
[63] Luke 8:48
[64] Luke 8:50

11

Jesus on Ophthalmology (1)

Matthew 9:27-34

As Jesus went on from there, two blind men followed him, crying loudly, 'Have mercy on us, Son of David!' When he entered the house, the blind men came to him; and Jesus said to them, 'Do you believe that I am able to do this?' They said to him, 'Yes, Lord.' Then he touched their eyes and said, 'According to your faith let it be done to you.' And their eyes were opened. Then Jesus sternly ordered them, 'See that no one knows of this.' But they went away and spread the news about him throughout that district.

After they had gone away, a demoniac who was mute was brought to him. And when the demon had been cast out, the one who had been mute spoke; and the crowds were amazed and said, 'Never has anything like this been seen in Israel.' But the Pharisees said, 'By the ruler of the demons he casts out the demons.'

An episode of the BBC series *Call the Midwife* featured a new mother who was blind and the encouragement and advice she was eventually able to get from a more experienced mother with the same disability.[65] The programme highlighted the greater sensitivity of other senses often experienced by those without sight, as well as the difficulties they face and the needs they have. Within the setting of 1960s Poplar in East London, there was also plenty of reference to the

---

[65] *Call the Midwife;* BBC1; 16 February 2020

rights of disabled people as human beings, even if they were not recognised in the same way as they are now.

Matthew puts this episode of two blind men near the end of two chapters of miracles and just before Jesus sends his disciples on a mission to do as he has been doing. Like many of the healings that precede this one, the subject of faith is an important factor.

Mentioning faith in the same paragraph as sight and blindness may also suggest the verse, *"We walk by faith, not by sight."*[66] The blind mothers in *Call the Midwife* found their way around by putting their faith in other senses, in a memory of how a room is laid out and in the guidance and help of others. What they relied upon was those things.

When Jesus says to the blind men in Matthew's account, *"According to your faith let it be done to you,"*[67] this is the principal sense in which he uses the word faith. It is not about the measure of their faith – how much of it they have – but the fact that they can rely upon him for this healing. He is the ophthalmic specialist they have been waiting for; he is the one they put their faith in.

But the story does raise another meaning of the word 'faith' that has at least equal weight in our thinking. Jesus asked them first, *"Do you believe that I am able to do this?"*[68] When we talk about our faith, what we often mean is the set of doctrinal principles that make up our system of belief. The question might, therefore, sound like, "Does your belief system include the possibility that I am a person with the power to give you sight?"

Given that Matthew's main purpose, in common with all the Gospel writers, is to show who Jesus is, we should include this sense of faith and belief along with the sense of reliance.

In any exploration of sight and blindness, it is hard to escape their use as a metaphor as well as literally. The saying 'there's none so blind as those who will not see' comes to mind. This is more thoroughly explored by the account of Jesus healing a man born blind in John chapter 9.[69] Taking the metaphorical aspect of sight and blindness in this passage leads us again to the context in which Matthew places it. The healing of two blind men comes near the end of two chapters of

---

[66] 2 Corinthians 5:7
[67] Matthew 9:29
[68] Matthew 9:28
[69] See chapter 16 on page 80

miracles, and immediately before the healing of a man with a demon whose symptoms were primarily an inability to talk. As so often happened with Jesus' actions and with the message about Jesus since his death and resurrection, there is a mixed reaction. The crowd were amazed and said, *"Nothing like this has ever been seen in Israel."*[70] But the Pharisees said, *"It is by the prince of demons that he drives out demons."*[71]

If Matthew's purpose is to show who Jesus is by describing what he did, this reaction indicates that some saw while others seemed blind. There are different levels of seeing in these circumstances when it is at least in part metaphorical. We may notice that something has happened but think nothing more of it. That would be like someone in the crowd being present and noticing that someone who apparently couldn't speak was now commenting on the weather.

Here it seems that the crowd took their sight to a deeper level. They saw that two blind men were now able to see, and a man who was unable to speak because of a demon was also cured, and they wondered at what was going on. On the basis of what they noticed, they asked the question which is sometimes made explicit: *"Who can this be?"*[72] or, *"What kind of man is this?"*[73]

The deepest level of sight – what we might call insight or realisation – is shown by the contrast between the blind men (who cannot see) and the Pharisees (who can). The blind men see who Jesus is, without the benefit of functioning eyesight, and realise what he can do for them. The Pharisees see the healing of the man who couldn't speak but can't make the connection with who Jesus must therefore be. They come up with a twisted argument about Jesus being an agent of the prince of demons. Matthew will return to this in chapter 12 after his next section of Jesus' teaching.[74]

It is the same choice that everyone has when confronted with what Jesus can do. He is either the chosen deliverer or he's working for the other side and covering his tracks with some double-dealing. Again, the context in which Matthew places the contrast is important. After

---

[70] Matthew 9:33
[71] Matthew 9:34
[72] Matthew 8:27 (NKJV)
[73] Matthew 8:27 (TNIV)
[74] Especially Matthew 12:22-37

chapter 9 comes chapter 10![75] In chapters 8 and 9 Jesus has shown his disciples and the crowds who he is by what he does, and he has shown his disciples the extent of the need. In chapter 10 he is about to send them on their own mission to *"heal those who are ill, raise the dead, cleanse those who have leprosy, drive out demons"*[76]. The negative reaction of the Pharisees to the healing of the man who couldn't speak shows them what they are up against.

We saw in the previous chapter, in relation to the woman healed of her condition of continuous menstruation, that it can be important to go public on what we ask of Jesus and the reliance we put on him. Here we see that even if we tell our stories of what Jesus has done for us, as the blind men did, we may get mixed reactions. If we don't *"spread the news about him"*[77], no one will have the opportunity to see – notice, wonder and realise – who he is.

---

[75] See note 8 on p.15
[76] Matthew 10:8
[77] Matthew 9:31

12

Jesus on Speech and Hearing Impairment

Mark 7:31-37

Then he returned from the region of Tyre, and went by way of Sidon towards the Sea of Galilee, in the region of the Decapolis. They brought to him a deaf man who had an impediment in his speech; and they begged him to lay his hand on him. He took him aside in private, away from the crowd, and put his fingers into his ears, and he spat and touched his tongue. Then looking up to heaven, he sighed and said to him, 'Ephphatha', that is, 'Be opened.' And immediately his ears were opened, his tongue was released, and he spoke plainly. Then Jesus ordered them to tell no one; but the more he ordered them, the more zealously they proclaimed it. They were astounded beyond measure, saying, 'He has done everything well; he even makes the deaf to hear and the mute to speak.'

Have you ever been shown something and told not to let anyone know you've seen it? Whether that was easy or difficult may have depended on what it was you were shown. Perhaps you have been told something 'in confidence' but it was such exciting news that you couldn't help sharing it with your partner or a friend.

Or perhaps you have experience of this the other way round. There's a piece of information that you want don't want spread around but it has to be shared with one individual. Because it is such good news for them, it is no time before you start to hear it everywhere you go.

This episode has silence, secrets and speech. The man is deaf and speaks as though his tongue is tied in knots, and then he hears and speaks plainly. Jesus tells everyone to keep quiet about it but they can't stop talking.

When we ask our usual question, "What's that all about, then?" there are (also as usual) clues in the story itself, as well as in the context, to the different levels at which we can read and receive the account.

On one level it is about the healing of a man who is deaf and unable to speak. It tells us that Jesus is someone able to heal a speech and hearing impairment. The means by which Mark records that Jesus performed this healing are reminiscent of other healers of the time, especially in pagan and Gentile traditions. Perhaps he includes these to assure Gentile readers that Jesus is someone who can do this kind of miracle, because he does it in a way they might expect.

All of this serves to point to another level of what this is all about. Jesus is someone who is able to heal a speech and hearing impairment whose power applies not just in the Jewish sphere but also the Gentile sphere. This extension of Jesus' ministry to the Gentile world is backed up by Mark's detail that this took place *"in the Decapolis"* – a predominantly Gentile region to the east of the Jordan.

This brings us to the most useful tool in our collection for interpretation. The context of this account points to more levels of what it may be all about. This story comes at the end of a series of miracles and teaching aimed at Jews, following the feeding of the five thousand. It comes immediately before the feeding of the four thousand and forms a bridge between the two series. Taken with the healing of the Syro-Phoenician woman's daughter, there is a transition from 'Jesus coming for Jews' to 'Jesus coming for Jews and Gentiles'.

It is paralleled with the healing of a blind man at Bethsaida[78] coming immediately before Jesus' question to his disciples as to who people say he is and who *they* say he is. The reactions of the crowds after this healing and after the healing of the blind man later are clearly

---

[78] Mark 8:22-26

meant to refer the reader to Isaiah 35, pointing out Jesus' fulfilment of prophecy.

"He has done everything well"[79] might even be meant as, "See how well he fulfils the prophecies."

It might be pushing Mark's intentions too far, but if we take Jesus' purpose as to proclaim and to embody the coming Kingdom of God, and if we take the prophecies to be about the nature of that Kingdom, and if we take God's eternal purpose as to renew creation by the establishment of his Kingdom, it is possible that *"He has done everything well"* might have echoes of Genesis 1:31 – *"God saw all that he had made, and it was very good."* If we're looking for it, this passage might even be pointing to Jesus as the inauguration of the new creation.

This might be the point at which you either think that I've pushed it too far and I'm becoming fanciful, or you might think, "That's all very interesting." Either way, you might also be thinking, "But why does Jesus command them not to tell anyone?"

Surely, we might think, a story about opening ears and loosening a tongue must be about people being able to hear and tell the great works of God. So, what's this secrecy all about, then? If we look at it the other way round, we might ask, "Why do these things if you don't want it known?"

Once again, we have to see Jesus' coming on two levels. To answer the second question first, Jesus comes for the individuals whom he meets. He engages with them; he meets their needs; he demonstrates his power and compassion and he makes them whole. It is part of his nature to do that; he cannot *not* act with love and compassion. The wonders of his love are naturally celebrated and proclaimed as individuals encounter them. People were overwhelmed with amazement when they saw and heard about the healing of the man with the speech and hearing impairment. They couldn't help celebrating and proclaiming that he had *"done everything well"*.

But Jesus also comes on a cosmic, global, eternal level as Israel's Messiah and the world's true Lord, to inaugurate the new creation by his life and ministry and especially by his death and resurrection. That had to be accomplished in a particular way in order to make all the

---

[79] Mark 7:37

right connections. If word about what he was doing got out and conclusions were drawn too early about who he was or who he thought he was, it was likely to precipitate a confrontation with the authorities.

So having been all round the text itself and seen it in its context, it is time to leap forward to the final aspect of its context, which is how we read and hear it now. It would be possible to be overwhelmed with amazement as we read and hear of the healing of a man with a speech and hearing impediment, but then see that Jesus commanded people not to tell anyone. We might conclude that we too are to keep quiet about the wonderful acts of God in our lives, either because Jesus said so or out of fear of provoking anger and controversy among our communities and authorities.

That conclusion would omit something very important. The confrontation that Jesus needed to avoid until the right time has now happened. The purpose of Jesus' life, ministry, death and resurrection has been accomplished and the new creation has been inaugurated. It is the role of those who associate with him, those who follow him and those who experience his continued work of healing and renewal, to have their eyes and ears opened and their tongues loosened so that they may speak plainly of the words and works of God.

Having our eyes and ears opened and our tongues loosened, we are called and sent *"to the ends of the earth"* to continue his work of opening eyes and ears and loosening tongues – the task being the same as Jesus' task of bringing God's Kingdom so that all may be renewed and all creation may say, *"He has done everything well."*

13

Jesus on Ophthalmology (2)

Mark 8:22-26

They came to Bethsaida. Some people brought a blind man to him and begged him to touch him. He took the blind man by the hand and led him out of the village; and when he had put saliva on his eyes and laid his hands on him, he asked him, 'Can you see anything?' And the man looked up and said, 'I can see people, but they look like trees, walking.' Then Jesus laid his hands on his eyes again; and he looked intently and his sight was restored, and he saw everything clearly. Then he sent him away to his home, saying, 'Do not even go into the village.'

Let's go straight to the context of this healing story. What comes before Mark 8:22? The answer, of course, is verse 21, which is Jesus' question to his disciples after some fairly cryptic comments about yeast and questions about the miracles of feeding five thousand and four thousand people. Jesus asked them, *"Do you still not understand?"*[80]

We might interpret *"understand"* with several parallels. He could have asked, "Don't you get it?" or, "Don't you see?" He might have wondered at their lack of insight or what else he needed to do or say to make it clearer.

In his account of Jesus' ministry with the purpose of describing and communicating the good news about Jesus the Messiah,[81] Mark follows the question about understanding with a story about healing a man who was blind.

---

[80] Mark 8:21
[81] Mark 1:1

In coming at the end of a section following the feeding of the four thousand, this story is parallel with the healing of the man with the speech and hearing impairment that we looked at in chapter 12. In both cases, the man is brought by an impersonal group of people and no one is named. There are two stages to the healing of the blind man, just as there were actions involved in the healing of the other. The purpose may be similar in demonstrating to formerly pagan or Gentile readers that Jesus was in the tradition of healers that they would recognise. Putting his hands on the man's eyes would also have been recognisable as the 'laying on of hands' to early Christians with gifts of healing.

It is part of Mark's purpose to show that Jesus' mission is about the Jews but it's not *just* about the Jews. There is clear reference to methods of healing that Greek readers would have recognised, but there is also clear reference to the fulfilment of Jewish scriptures, especially Isaiah 35.

Then will the eyes of the blind be opened,
and the ears of the deaf unstopped.
Then will the lame leap like a deer,
and the mute tongue shout for joy.[82]

So, as with healing of the other blind men, it seems to be about opening the eyes of insight as well as the physical eyes of this blind man. This is especially clear when we look at the context in the other direction. What comes after verse 26?

No doubt you're ahead of me and shouting, "Verse 27!" This is Jesus' question to the disciples about who people say that he is, followed by the direct question, *"But what about you? Who do you say I am?"*[83] He's finding out if they've had any further insight because of the healing of a blind man since their earlier lack of understanding. At that point Peter is able to answer, *"You are the Messiah..."*

This should not be overinterpreted as an understanding of Jesus' divinity. This would come later. But it is a deeper insight than they had earlier in their very physical discussions about bread, and it is a deeper insight than the crowds' opinions that Jesus was a prophetic figure like Elijah or John the Baptist. The implication is that Peter had reached

---

[82] Isaiah 35:5-6
[83] Mark 8:29 (TNIV)

that realisation through what he had seen and heard and the work of the Spirit in revealing it to him. Jesus had made it clear that there was something to understand but he had not spelt out what answer they were meant to give.

It seems that might be part of the answer to the question of secrecy that we addressed in chapter 12. Like Peter, we are to seek the revelation and insight from the Spirit rather than expect to be told who Jesus is. But Jesus' command to secrecy is still not applicable to us, as we live after the time when his mission and purpose has been accomplished. This is finally spelt out for Peter, James and John when they have seen an even clearer manifestation of who Jesus is on the Mount of Transfiguration in the next chapter.[84] *"Jesus gave them orders not to tell anyone what they had seen until the Son of Man had risen from the dead."*[85]

It is now time that those who have heard and seen shall have their tongues loosened to tell the wonders of God that others may also have revealed to them who Jesus is.

---

[84] Mark 9:2-9
[85] Mark 2:9

14

Jesus on Possession (3)

Luke 11:14-28

Now he was casting out a demon that was mute; when the demon had gone out, the one who had been mute spoke, and the crowds were amazed. But some of them said, 'He casts out demons by Beelzebul, the ruler of the demons.' Others, to test him, kept demanding from him a sign from heaven. But he knew what they were thinking and said to them, 'Every kingdom divided against itself becomes a desert, and house falls on house. If Satan also is divided against himself, how will his kingdom stand? — for you say that I cast out the demons by Beelzebul. Now if I cast out the demons by Beelzebul, by whom do your exorcists cast them out? Therefore they will be your judges. But if it is by the finger of God that I cast out the demons, then the kingdom of God has come to you. When a strong man, fully armed, guards his castle, his property is safe. But when one stronger than he attacks him and overpowers him, he takes away his armour in which he trusted and divides his plunder. Whoever is not with me is against me, and whoever does not gather with me scatters.

'When the unclean spirit has gone out of a person, it wanders through waterless regions looking for a resting-place, but not finding any, it says, "I will return to my house from which I came." When it comes, it finds it swept and put in order. Then it goes and brings seven other spirits more evil than itself, and they enter and live there; and the last state of that person is worse than the first.'

While he was saying this, a woman in the crowd raised her voice and said to him, 'Blessed is the womb that bore you and the breasts that nursed you!' But he said, 'Blessed rather are those who hear the word of God and obey it!'

For the first few weeks of lockdown during the Coronavirus pandemic, many people went outside their front doors at 8pm on Thursdays to applaud the NHS and key workers who put themselves at risk to treat others and to provide essential services. We recognised acts of self-sacrifice and of healing which brought the community and the nation together. This was a healthy antidote for a time in which some people had been panic-stockpiling toilet rolls and flour, and we could have disintegrated into chaos and anarchy if the spirit of 'everyone for themselves' had been allowed to take over.

Applause is the way we typically express our appreciation. In Jesus' day it would have been similarly common to express appreciation for someone by saying, *"Blessed is the mother who gave you birth and nursed you."*[86] Applause and appreciation, expressed in whatever way is culturally appropriate, is a good thing. Nowhere does Jesus say that we shouldn't give praise and express gratitude where it is deserved. But Jesus also doesn't waste an opportunity to add to the message he had been bringing through the previous conversation.

Yes, healing the man with the demon so he could speak was a good action, and what he said afterwards were wise and helpful words. The applause is deserved. But Jesus says, gratitude and appreciation should go further. He might be paraphrased as saying that 'actions speak louder than words' – or applause for that matter. If you see good things done, the best way to demonstrate appreciation is to join in. *"Blessed rather are those who hear the word of God and obey it."*[87]

All of this reinforces on the national and global level what Jesus has been doing and talking about on the individual level, because of the controversy after the healing of a man with a demon that couldn't speak.

With modern medical, psychological and psychiatric knowledge, we would not so easily attribute the cause of an inability to speak to a demon. We would probably diagnose a form of mental illness where

---

[86] Luke 11:27
[87] Luke 11:28

the fear and anxiety had so affected this man that he found he couldn't express himself. The kind of trauma that may have caused such a condition is hard to imagine by those who have not experienced something similar.

On the individual level, Jesus demonstrated that the power of the God of love is greater than the power of the trauma that robbed him of his speech.

Jesus' critics seek to discredit him with a disingenuous accusation of being an undercover agent for the power of evil that seeks to steal and kill and destroy. Jesus points out the faults in their logic. The destructive forces of the kind of trauma that caused this man's inability to speak are not likely to be the source of the cure. Jesus goes on to underline the purpose of his life and ministry which will be accomplished in his death and resurrection. He comes to establish a beach head in the liberation of enemy-occupied territory. Jesus' purpose is to establish God's Kingdom of life and love and wholeness where there is death, destruction and disintegration.

On the individual level, Jesus raises the question for us of what we rely upon for our protection and our wholeness. Do we rely upon the power of God and the ways of life and love expressed in the service of others? Or do we seek refuge in the ways and habits that actually lead to breakdown of health, relationships or personality?

Jesus points out that the demon – that which destroys and disintegrates – is not the source of healing even if it can create the illusion of safety and security. It is only the power of God that ultimately makes us whole.

All this works on the individual level, in relation to the conversation about casting out the demon or healing the result of this man's particular trauma. But, as always, Jesus is never just talking about an individual and the healing of their particular condition. Jesus' favourite topic was the Kingdom of God. He seldom opened his mouth without mentioning it, even if the actual words didn't pass his lips on every occasion. The Kingdom of God is always relevant on the communal, national, global and even cosmic and eternal levels.

Enemy-occupied territory applies not just to individual minds and bodies gripped by disease and the results of trauma or abuse. Enemy-occupied territory also applies to the community and the nation where the ways of corruption and duplicity dominate at the inevitable expense of the poor, the weak, those born without privilege and those without 'friends in high places'.

On this level, Jesus is straight to the point and very direct: *"...whoever is not with me is against me."*[88] It has been well interpreted as, "All that is required for evil to triumph is for good people to do nothing."[89]

Those who hear the word of God and obey it by bringing healing and peace, joy and wholeness, justice, compassion and love are worth more in the growth of God's Kingdom than those who simply applaud but do nothing.

---

[88] Luke 11:23
[89] A quotation variously attributed in its original to Edmund Burke or to John Stuart Mill.

15

Jesus on Ophthalmology (3)

John 9

As he walked along, he saw a man blind from birth. His disciples asked him, 'Rabbi, who sinned, this man or his parents, that he was born blind?' Jesus answered, 'Neither this man nor his parents sinned; he was born blind so that God's works might be revealed in him. We must work the works of him who sent me while it is day; night is coming when no one can work. As long as I am in the world, I am the light of the world.' When he had said this, he spat on the ground and made mud with the saliva and spread the mud on the man's eyes, saying to him, 'Go, wash in the pool of Siloam' (which means Sent). Then he went and washed and came back able to see. The neighbours and those who had seen him before as a beggar began to ask, 'Is this not the man who used to sit and beg?' Some were saying, 'It is he.' Others were saying, 'No, but it is someone like him.' He kept saying, 'I am the man.' But they kept asking him, 'Then how were your eyes opened?' He answered, 'The man called Jesus made mud, spread it on my eyes, and said to me, "Go to Siloam and wash." Then I went and washed and received my sight.' They said to him, 'Where is he?' He said, 'I do not know.'

They brought to the Pharisees the man who had formerly been blind. Now it was a sabbath day when Jesus made the mud and opened his eyes. Then the Pharisees also began to ask him how he had received his sight. He said to them, 'He put mud on my eyes. Then I washed, and now I see.' Some of the Pharisees said,

75

'This man is not from God, for he does not observe the sabbath.' But others said, 'How can a man who is a sinner perform such signs?' And they were divided. So they said again to the blind man, 'What do you say about him? It was your eyes he opened.' He said, 'He is a prophet.'

The Jews did not believe that he had been blind and had received his sight until they called the parents of the man who had received his sight and asked them, 'Is this your son, who you say was born blind? How then does he now see?' His parents answered, 'We know that this is our son, and that he was born blind; but we do not know how it is that now he sees, nor do we know who opened his eyes. Ask him; he is of age. He will speak for himself.' His parents said this because they were afraid of the Jews; for the Jews had already agreed that anyone who confessed Jesus to be the Messiah would be put out of the synagogue. Therefore his parents said, 'He is of age; ask him.'

So for the second time they called the man who had been blind, and they said to him, 'Give glory to God! We know that this man is a sinner.' He answered, 'I do not know whether he is a sinner. One thing I do know, that though I was blind, now I see.' They said to him, 'What did he do to you? How did he open your eyes?' He answered them, 'I have told you already, and you would not listen. Why do you want to hear it again? Do you also want to become his disciples?' Then they reviled him, saying, 'You are his disciple, but we are disciples of Moses. We know that God has spoken to Moses, but as for this man, we do not know where he comes from.' The man answered, 'Here is an astonishing thing! You do not know where he comes from, and yet he opened my eyes. We know that God does not listen to sinners, but he does listen to one who worships him and obeys his will. Never since the world began has it been heard that anyone opened the eyes of a person born blind. If this man were not from God, he could do nothing.' They answered him, 'You were born entirely in sins, and are you trying to teach us?' And they drove him out.

Jesus heard that they had driven him out, and when he found him, he said, 'Do you believe in the Son of Man?' He answered, 'And who is he, sir? Tell me, so that I may believe in him.' Jesus said to him, 'You have seen him, and the one speaking with you is he.' He said, 'Lord, I believe.' And he worshipped him. Jesus said, 'I came into this world for judgement so that those who do not see may see, and those who do see may become blind.' Some of the Pharisees near him heard this and said to him, 'Surely we are not blind, are we?' Jesus said to them, 'If you were blind, you would not have sin. But now that you say, "We see", your sin remains.'

Sometimes when people are suffering illness, disability or some other adversity, they ask, "What have I done to deserve this?" Of course, actions do have consequences. Gratitude is often the result of kindness. Similarly, bad things can be the result of bad actions. People get killed and injured on the roads because of lack of care and attention. But it is also true to say that many speeding drivers get away with it.

It is not a new idea that our sufferings might be the result of the bad actions of ourselves or someone else. Apparently, innocent suffering has been a philosophical conundrum for a long time and is the subject of the Book of Job. The question, "Why do bad things happen to good people?" is answered by the statement, "Because bad things happen to people." But still people say, "I must have been very wicked in a previous life to have ended up like this."

Perhaps we should listen more carefully to what Jesus had to say when asked a version of the same question in relation to a man who had been born blind. *"Who sinned, this man or his parents, that he was born blind?"*[90]

Jesus' answer is unequivocal: *"...neither..."*[91]

Helpfully, Jesus goes on. He does not simply express an insight that this disability may have come from another source. Jesus says that disability and illness should not be put beside a desire to attribute blame. Disability and illness should be put beside a desire to see the word and works of God. Disability and illness, along with death as we

---

[90] John 9:2
[91] John 9:3

shall see when we come to Lazarus' grave in John 11, are part of the nature of a world of darkness and chaos which is not the way it is meant to be.

John is using this account of healing a man born blind to pursue his bigger theme of light and darkness. The healing becomes a sign as he reveals more of who Jesus is and how people come to believe in him. The works of God are done in the light of day just as God's creative work was done in the light. But night is coming, when Jesus will not be in the world, following his death and burial.[92] While he is in the world, Jesus is the light of the world that gives light to everyone, though he is not received and recognised by everyone.[93]

In this chapter Jesus speaks at the beginning and the end, but even when he has disappeared in the middle, he remains the focus. The question is about identity. Firstly, the identity of the man formerly blind is called into question. It is really a way of hiding the question of the identity of Jesus. If the man has not actually been healed, because he's a different man, the neighbours and Pharisees don't have to grapple with the identity of a person who could heal a man born blind.

When it is confirmed that he has been blind but can now see, the religious structures and rules are challenged because the healing took place on a Sabbath. It is left to the once blind man to work through the questions about the identity of the person who healed him: he's a prophet; he's a healer. But according to the Pharisees, he can't be from God because he did what he did on the Sabbath. Elsewhere, Jesus suggests that people following that kind of reasoning should read the prophets and learn what it means that God desires *"mercy not sacrifice"*[94].

John's references to being put out of the synagogue probably refer not just to the blind man but also to the church after Jesus' time being put out of the synagogue. This makes the parallel between the blind man and Jesus' followers seeing and recognising the ways of God and being cut off from their community and isolated as a result. It is in this position that Jesus finds the blind man and he comes to the fulness of belief.

---

[92] John 13:30
[93] John 1:9-10
[94] Hosea 6:6, quoted by Jesus in Matthew 9:13

Through the earlier interrogations he has progressed from Jesus simply being *"a man"* through asserting that Jesus is a prophet and healer. Jesus asks him directly about his belief in the Son of Man.

From reading the Gospels, we know that this was Jesus' favourite way of talking about himself, but the once blind man didn't know that. He would have recognised the title as coming from the Book of Daniel, referring to one who would be raised to the throne of judgement next to God, when all things would be made right and new as the evils of the world would be overcome and God's reign established.

This man's belief in Jesus as the Son of Man stems from Jesus giving him sight where there had never been sight before. He brought the light of sight into the dark chaos of this man's entire existence up to that point. For John, it could hardly have been a clearer statement that Jesus comes to usher in the beginnings of the new creation and the triumph of light and life, grace and truth over darkness, chaos, death and deceit.

It turns out that some Pharisees were around when Jesus was having this conversation with the newly sighted man, which gives him the opportunity to reiterate the teaching in response to the disciples' original question. Those who are blind are not to be blamed; those who claim to see – or understand – when they are actually blind or deceiving themselves are guilty.

16

Jesus on Possession (4)

Mark 9:14-29

When they came to the disciples, they saw a great crowd around them, and some scribes arguing with them. When the whole crowd saw him, they were immediately overcome with awe, and they ran forward to greet him. He asked them, 'What are you arguing about with them?' Someone from the crowd answered him, 'Teacher, I brought you my son; he has a spirit that makes him unable to speak; and whenever it seizes him, it dashes him down; and he foams and grinds his teeth and becomes rigid; and I asked your disciples to cast it out, but they could not do so.' He answered them, 'You faithless generation, how much longer must I be among you? How much longer must I put up with you? Bring him to me.' And they brought the boy to him. When the spirit saw him, immediately it threw the boy into convulsions, and he fell on the ground and rolled about, foaming at the mouth. Jesus asked the father, 'How long has this been happening to him?' And he said, 'From childhood. It has often cast him into the fire and into the water, to destroy him; but if you are able to do anything, have pity on us and help us.' Jesus said to him, 'If you are able!—All things can be done for the one who believes.' Immediately the father of the child cried out, 'I believe; help my unbelief!' When Jesus saw that a crowd came running together, he rebuked the unclean spirit, saying to it, 'You spirit that keep this boy from speaking and hearing, I command you, come out of him, and never enter him again!' After crying out and convulsing him terribly, it came out, and the boy was like a corpse, so that most of them said, 'He is dead.' But Jesus took him by the hand and lifted him up, and he was able to stand. When he had entered the house, his disciples asked him privately, 'Why could we not cast it out?' He said to them, 'This kind can come out only through prayer.'

In most jobs there are likely to be tasks that become fairly routine, but as they're all slightly different, there may be an occasion when one becomes particularly difficult. After the usual initial assessment, it becomes apparent that this instance is much more difficult than usual.

That seems to be the experience of the disciples in this passage. They've been used to having authority over evil spirits, driving out demons and healing people.[95] The symptoms described twice by the father of this boy indicate epilepsy, and the disciples had found themselves unable to heal him.

Modern medical, psychiatric and psychological knowledge enables us to diagnose diseases of the body and mind much more precisely. Attributing everything to different forms of spirit doesn't fit with this modern approach, but does help us to see that all diseases are part of the nature of a world that is not perfect in the way it was intended and originally created to be.

Jesus' close identification with God, which has been revealed to three of the disciples in the Transfiguration immediately preceding this event, is also revealed in his reaction to the news that this spirit had proved too powerful for the other nine. It is as though Jesus groans at their inability to see the immediate presence of God's power and glory to rule over all things.

In the narrative as Mark tells it, Jesus first asks for another description of the symptoms, before engaging in a discussion about faith with the boy's father while his son continues to writhe on the ground foaming at the mouth. In the conversation there are two exclamations from the father that may be echoed by many people.

This father is desperate; his son has suffered these fits with near fatal consequences all his life. The father cries out, *"If you can do anything, take pity on us and help us."* It is left to us to imagine where he puts the emphasis:

---

95 Mark 6:7,13

1. *If* you can do anything...

2. If *you* can do anything...

3. If you can do *anything*...

And what is his tone? Is it desperation? Is there a sense of resignation that perhaps his last hope will not be fruitful?

But Jesus puts the ball back in his court. *"If you can?"* said Jesus. *"Everything is possible for one who believes."*[96]

The father realises he's come to a point where what he has to do is far more difficult than anything he's encountered before, and he says something many of us may have echoed before. *"I do believe; help me overcome my unbelief!"*[97]

There is much that might make us wonder about the nature of faith and belief. To many of us, whatever faith we have may seem woefully inadequate next to the size of the obstacle in front of us. It hardly seems encouraging that Jesus' comment associated with this incident in Matthew's account is, *"If you have faith as small as a mustard seed, you can say to this mountain, 'Move from here to there,' and it will move."*[98]

It leaves us with the conclusion that when people we pray for are not healed, there must be something lacking in our faith. Maybe our faith is not even the size of a mustard seed. When we read Jesus' answer to the disciples that *"this kind can only come out by prayer"*, we may think there's something lacking in our prayer.

There is certainly much in Jesus' words and actions that is a response to faith in those he encounters, and he certainly laments the lack of faith in the whole generation.[99] But perhaps we should not be so hard on ourselves. God is compassionate and merciful. The Gospel writers wrote with the overriding purpose of showing who Jesus is and how his life, ministry, death and resurrection inaugurate the new creation. The accounts of healings are part of the means of demonstrating this. They are not meant to show that anyone who asks in the right way or has a certain level of faith or engages in the right

---

96 Mark 9:23
97 Mark 9:24
98 Matthew 17:20
99 Mark 9:19

spiritual practices and disciplines will have instant healing from any and every condition and disease.

If we put the overriding purpose of the Gospel as a whole next to this story, we can be more aware of the clues. Jesus laments the lack of belief in that generation because even though they have the embodiment of God's Kingdom among them, they cannot see it. The father represents those who want to see it but find it hard to hold firmly to that when things are hard.

It may be pushing interpretation too far, but perhaps it is also possible to see the attitude of God the Father in the father of the boy. Perhaps there is a hint of the grieving love of the Father for his child, Israel? Or for his image-bearing children throughout the world? Perhaps there is also the grief of the Father for his unique Son, Jesus, as he goes silently to a certain death?

All of that is true, and if we choose to see it reflected in the father of a boy with the spirit of epilepsy, then it shows us something of God, even if Mark didn't write it with that intent.

The part of the story that really points us to the purpose of Jesus' life, ministry, death and resurrection in inaugurating the new creation is the healing of the boy. We've left him writhing on the ground, as they did throughout their discussions, but finally Jesus commanded the spirit to come out of him and never return. His final convulsion was not the end of the story, even though most people would have said that he was dead.

"Jesus took him by the hand and lifted him to his feet, and he stood up."[100] It might be better, if less descriptive, to say, "Jesus took him by the hand and *raised him up* and he arose." Both words are commonly used in the New Testament in reference to resurrection. Most people would have said that he was dead, just as Jairus' daughter had been dead. Here we see the new creation breaking into the old.

So, we echo the disciples' question when we have a chance to talk among ourselves and to ask Jesus why our faith seems to fall so far short that we are unable to heal every time we're asked. *"Why couldn't we drive it out?"* Why are we not able to participate sufficiently in the presence of the Kingdom of God, so that all that is wrong with a world of disease, destruction and death disappear as soon as we speak?

---

[100] Mark 9:27

Jesus says that *"this kind can only come out by prayer"*. And we reply that we thought we *were* praying, as we had been for the previous healings.

Perhaps there are two lessons to be taken from this.

1. When Jesus speaks of prayer in this instance, maybe there is a particular closeness to God that is envisaged. Presumably the Transfiguration had been a particularly intense spiritual connection that was needed to bring the power of the Kingdom to bear upon a boy in such a state.

2. It says to us that our walk with Jesus can get especially difficult at any stage. The obstacles on our spiritual journey can cause us to stop and question how we can continue. The lesson is not to take it for granted. There is no magic formula. Jesus never said it would be easy, but told us to take up our cross daily and follow him.

17

Jesus on Disability (3)

Luke 13:10-17

Now he was teaching in one of the synagogues on the sabbath. And just then there appeared a woman with a spirit that had crippled her for eighteen years. She was bent over and was quite unable to stand up straight. When Jesus saw her, he called her over and said, 'Woman, you are set free from your ailment.' When he laid his hands on her, immediately she stood up straight and began praising God. But the leader of the synagogue, indignant because Jesus had cured on the sabbath, kept saying to the crowd, 'There are six days on which work ought to be done; come on those days and be cured, and not on the sabbath day.' But the Lord answered him and said, 'You hypocrites! Does not each of you on the sabbath untie his ox or his donkey from the manger, and lead it away to give it water? And ought not this woman, a daughter of Abraham whom Satan bound for eighteen long years, be set free from this bondage on the sabbath day?' When he said this, all his opponents were put to shame; and the entire crowd was rejoicing at all the wonderful things that he was doing.

It seems to be human nature to try to find our way around the rules imposed by a system if they are inconvenient to us. We go to great lengths to justify our decisions. During the restrictions imposed for the COVID-19 pandemic, I found myself justifying a decision to travel further for a walk than was allowed, on the basis that it was not the distance that you travelled that transmitted the virus but the contacts with people, and I could have more of those on a walk near to home than on a walk further away. Other, more serious breaches of the rules, also took place on the basis of a balance of risks. People also worked out which of two actions was a lesser of two evils: breaking the rules or caring for the wellbeing of a loved one. Others dutifully kept to the rules and endured much grief and inconvenience, in the belief that it was for the benefit of all and that everyone was following the rules. It is not surprising that they were angry when they found out that many who made the rules were not keeping them in the same way and that the breaking of them was for less selfless reasons.

While at synagogue one Sabbath, Jesus is faced with a similar dilemma: to treat the disabled woman who is there in front of him or to keep the Sabbath regulations and arrange to meet the following day.

The implications of his decision are spelt out for us, as Luke gives his account of the encounter. Healing the woman would be breaking Sabbath regulations and earn him the indignation of the synagogue leader. It also earned him the delight and wonder of the congregation and probably the rest of the town – to say nothing of the woman herself.

If he had not healed her, the synagogue leader would probably have taken it for granted and not really noticed something not being done. Presumably there had been several Sabbaths during the eighteen years that this woman had suffered her crippling disability. No one rejoiced every week when she wasn't healed on an inappropriate day. Similarly, probably the rest of the congregation would not have been indignant that Jesus didn't heal her. Something *not* happening is seldom remarkable, either for those who would rejoice to see it happen or for those who would be indignant to see it happen.

Presumably Jesus could calculate that he would earn just as much delight and wonder from the people of the town if he healed her the next day. It might be possible to construct a case for a Sunday being a more appropriate day to give her the new start that she needed. Maybe that is to read it with Christian, post-resurrection eyes, but it would fit with the idea of a new creation beginning for her on the first day of the new week after eighteen years of struggle.

Equally, we might want to say that the Sabbath is an appropriate day to give her rest from the struggles of eighteen years battling with disability that meant she was bent over by the weight of her condition.

Perhaps Jesus could see both possibilities. And perhaps he knew that to argue over it was not the point. Jesus is always the practitioner of love. When asked on another occasion about who the neighbour is who is to be loved, his answer was the story of the Samaritan who demonstrated love and care for the man who had been robbed and beaten on the road.[101] The point he makes is that the neighbour we are to love is the person who is at hand who is in need.

On this occasion, in this synagogue, this woman is standing in front of him having endured eighteen years of crippling disability. He probably by-passed the question "Who is my neighbour?" and jumped straight to the conclusion that this woman was in need of a demonstration of God's love and care. He put his hands on her, and immediately she straightened up and praised God.

We've been looking at this as Jesus weighing up the 'greater of two goods' (rather than the lesser of two evils). In this way, it becomes another practical answer to the question, "Which is the greatest commandment?" Keeping the Sabbath holy, with all the human regulations that have been imposed as interpretation of what it means to keep a day 'holy', comes some way behind loving his neighbour.

But there's more to it than that. Another point that Jesus brings out in his answer to the synagogue leader is the hypocrisy of those who find their way around the regulations when it suits them but are quick to impose them on others. One rule for some and another for others is not a basis on which to build a community of God's people.

Jesus is asking us to consider that if there's a good reason for us to break some rules, should we not also consider another person's reasons and see that they are just as good as ours (perhaps even better)? Having that pointed out certainly made Jesus' opponents stop and think, such that they were humiliated.

We've already looked at the frequent diagnosis in the Gospels that a person's physical condition is the result of a demon or a spirit. Whether you see it literally this way, or think that it is more likely that it is the physical result of an injury or a medical or psychological condition, doesn't alter the end result. In this instance, whatever the actual physical or spiritual cause, this woman has been severely

---

[101] Luke 10:25-37

restricted in her movement and mobility for eighteen years. Because of that, the issue that this incident raises is one of freedom.

Whether it is purely a physical condition, or if there is a spiritual cause to it, her freedom is restricted. She has not been able to stand up straight in the appropriate posture for praise and worship in the synagogue. She has not been able to do many of the things that would make her more fully human; she has been bent double, looking towards the ground rather than up towards her maker and her God.

Always the one to see what would make someone whole and bring them a fullness of life, Jesus knew that God's loving, creative actions would be to bring her the freedom of a life of praise and worship. He put his hands on her and immediately she straightened up and praised God.

This daughter of Abraham, a member of God's people who was able to access the synagogue in spite of her disability, had been unable to participate fully in their worship. Jesus reached out and touched her. There is no implication that to touch her might have been inappropriate for any reason, but it is possible that it is the first time she has been touched in a caring way by anyone outside the home in a very long time. It is enough to set her free. She is free to be the person God made her to be within the community of God's people.

The challenge is to ensure that our rules, regulations and restrictions – however well intentioned – are not preventing people from entering fully into the life and worship of God's people.

- Are there ways in which our churches, our communities or our nations exclude and restrict others who should be able to participate?

- Are the ways in which we treat our domestic animals, or even our machinery, better than the ways we treat other members of the community?

It may be that we can't see that anything we do could really make a difference, but allowing our eyes to wander to the next verse after this passage, we see that Jesus goes on to make two comparisons to explain what the Kingdom of God is like.

In this context, after healing a disabled woman, Jesus goes on to ask, *"What is the Kingdom of God like?"* Jesus does not waste the opportunity to remind those present that what he is all about is the growth of God's Kingdom. Each act of healing contributes to the growth of the Kingdom. The implication is that whatever little we do in giving freedom and inclusion will influence and help to build the Kingdom in our communities.

18

Jesus on Leprosy (2)

Luke 17:11-19

On the way to Jerusalem Jesus was going through the region between Samaria and Galilee. As he entered a village, ten lepers approached him. Keeping their distance, they called out, saying, 'Jesus, Master, have mercy on us!' When he saw them, he said to them, 'Go and show yourselves to the priests.' And as they went, they were made clean. Then one of them, when he saw that he was healed, turned back, praising God with a loud voice. He prostrated himself at Jesus' feet and thanked him. And he was a Samaritan. Then Jesus asked, 'Were not ten made clean? But the other nine, where are they? Was none of them found to return and give praise to God except this foreigner?' Then he said to him, 'Get up and go on your way; your faith has made you well.'

It seems that these ten men were an isolated support bubble. They all had a notifiable disease of the skin which may or may not have been leprosy but was treated as extremely contagious. It is estimated that someone with leprosy was required to keep not two metres' but fifty metres' distance from anyone else. The condition that these men shared on the border between Samaria and Galilee was enough to overcome what would otherwise have kept them apart.

In all other aspects of life, that border would have been a 'hard border'; Jews and Samaritans didn't associate with one another,[102] but the shared condition of leprosy, with its requirement to isolate, meant

---

[102] John 4:9

those religious and political divisions were overcome in the interests of a solidarity in suffering. Their affliction brought them together. They had companionship and perhaps the camaraderie that goes with being a group of ten men together. But they probably also had the frustrations of their companions always being the same and the restrictions of being unable to be part of the activities of the rest of the community. Added to the effects of their isolation were the effects of the disease itself in their discomfort, the deterioration of their condition and the pain that would have gone with it.

At first reading it may seem natural that they called out from their fifty-metres safe distance, *"Jesus, Master, have pity on us!"*

But I wonder if it was such a natural thing to say. They may have called out for pity from any passers-by in the expectation of being given money as a contribution to living expenses. But they don't seem to be asking for pity for their economic situation. They seem to know Jesus' name and they call him *"Master"*. There's something in that call, keeping their required distance, that indicates that here is someone who can do more than relieve the anxiety around how they might afford to eat that day.

Certainly, Jesus chooses to interpret their request that way. Jesus doesn't do a skin specialist's consultation: he doesn't ask about symptoms; he doesn't check out what their condition is; he doesn't want to inspect their skin to see how bad the leprosy is. Jesus doesn't do a money advice or benefits consultation either – he doesn't enquire about their financial situation. There is neither means testing nor medical examination to assess the need. Jesus simply recognises that they believe he can help them, and tells them to go and do what they were required to do as if they had been cured.

At the beginning of his account of this episode, Luke has reminded us that Jesus is on his way to Jerusalem, but being on the border between Galilee and Samaria means that he still had some way to go. When Jesus told the ten people suffering the effects of leprosy to show themselves to the priests, he was probably referring to someone locally rather than the priests at the temple in Jerusalem.

They went without question, so Jesus' response must have been what they were hoping for. If they'd wanted a financial contribution, they might have hesitated or expressed some doubts about whether that was really a good idea. They went, and as they went, they were cleansed. We're not told what the ratio of Jews and Samaritans in the group was, but the implication of the situation being on the borders between Galilee and Samaria is that there was a mixture.

There are two points to make out of the return of one Samaritan to express his gratitude. One is to do with him being a Samaritan, but first let's think about gratitude.

If you stop for a moment and think about what you're grateful for, you might find you don't ever finish this chapter(!), but you might also realise that you perhaps haven't expressed that gratitude very often. There are many things in life which we are grateful for if we stop and think about it. Some of those are day-to-day occurrences which we might say 'thank you' for in a fairly automatic way. Others we may never actually express our thanks for at all. It can be a good spiritual discipline to count our blessings and give thanks to God and to the human agents who give us good things and do kind things for us.

But in terms of gratitude, it is less surprising that this Samaritan came back to thank Jesus as God's agent in cleansing him of his leprosy than that the other nine didn't. Perhaps they were all Jews and wanted to do the right thing under the law first, and by the time the priest had certified their cure, Jesus had moved on. Or perhaps they were so overjoyed that they went home to share time and celebrations with family, friends and neighbours from whom they'd been isolating for quite some time, and they never thought to go to the person who had apparently been so instrumental in their change of circumstances.

What is clear in the way Luke tells the story is that it is good to express the gratitude that is felt to the one who is responsible.

It may be that the reason one came back to give thanks is connected to the mixed nature of the group. Perhaps the change of circumstances meant that the Jews among them – up to all of the other nine – no longer needed to associate with a Samaritan because they no longer had their disease in common. An important point that Luke is making by stressing that it was a Samaritan who returned to give thanks and that this was on the border between Samaria and Galilee is that Jesus had established *medicine sans frontiers*.

In Jesus' scheme of things – the ways of God's kingdom – it is not just illness that brings people together, but healing and wholeness that extends from the individual to the community and on to the whole of humanity. There are no borders in the Kingdom of God. God's love and mercy – the pity that these ten people asked for – extends beyond the borders that human beings erect between nations and races, the sick and the healthy, the able and the disabled; and between the people 'like us' and the people who are 'not like us'.

Jesus' final comment is to make reference to the former leper's faith. This is not in contrast to the other nine. All ten were cleansed so all ten had faith, because all ten called out and asked for pity. Luke tells it this way to underline the faith of the outsider, who has been included simply because he was part of a group that expressed faith in terms of their trust and reliance on Jesus to help them.

There's a model here for our faith.

Do we call out to Jesus asking for pity when in circumstances over which we have little or no control? Is that an expression of faith, in that we believe he is Lord and Master of all things and we can rely on him for that mercy and help?

When we receive mercy and help, do we return to give thanks to God through Jesus and any other human agents that he might send to help us?

And finally, do we realise the importance for us of Jesus' instruction to the Samaritan former leper, *"Rise and go"*?

As we've noted before, the word translated 'rise' would have been familiar to Luke's readers among the early Christian community as being related to the word for resurrection. When God in Christ transforms our circumstances – even across seemingly impermeable human borders – he calls us into the new creation of the one who has been raised from the dead. Being told to *"Rise and go"* is to be told to become part of the new creation and live the life of the Kingdom across borders of geography, society, politics and culture.

19

Jesus on Ophthalmology (4)

Mark 10:46-52

They came to Jericho. As he and his disciples and a large crowd were leaving Jericho, Bartimaeus son of Timaeus, a blind beggar, was sitting by the roadside. When he heard that it was Jesus of Nazareth, he began to shout out and say, 'Jesus, Son of David, have mercy on me!' Many sternly ordered him to be quiet, but he cried out even more loudly, 'Son of David, have mercy on me!' Jesus stood still and said, 'Call him here.' And they called the blind man, saying to him, 'Take heart; get up, he is calling you.' So throwing off his cloak, he sprang up and came to Jesus. Then Jesus said to him, 'What do you want me to do for you?' The blind man said to him, 'My teacher, let me see again.' Jesus said to him, 'Go; your faith has made you well.' Immediately he regained his sight and followed him on the way.

In many ways it's a day like any other: quite unremarkable – hot, dry and dusty. It's always hot, dry and dusty in Jericho. But there's one thing that makes this day different. There's something of a celebrity coming to town. We've heard about Jesus of Nazareth. Stories of some of the things he's said and done have come ahead of him. Yesterday there was a rumour that he was heading for Jerusalem and was likely to pass this way today.

We've come out to see. Someone had gone out early to see if he was on his way and, hearing the message that he is, we've all come out to see. I want to understand what the fuss is all about. Has he really been healing people from long-term and life-threatening conditions and diseases? I wonder if he'll do anything like that here in Jericho.

It seems the whole town is lining the streets and there's quite a noise going on, with people shouting and pushing, trying to get a good view. Then there's a voice shouting above the noise of the crowd. I recognise Bartimaeus. He's near the back of the crowd; he's sitting on his cloak. Bartimaeus can't see and he sits by the roadside begging. He always has his cloak with him but I don't think I've ever seen him wear it. It's just for people to put money in. Poor old Bartimaeus can't see... so he can't work... so he can't earn a living. He's dependent on what people give him. Most of us know Bartimaeus and most of us put a bit in his cloak from time to time.

Bartimaeus is calling out; he's asked what's going on, having heard the hubbub, and someone has told him that Jesus of Nazareth is on his way into town; if he's on his way to Jerusalem, he'll only be another couple of days on the way. Bartimaeus is calling out above the noise of the crowd, and my excitement is tinged with a moment of hesitation and caution. Bartimaeus called Jesus *"Son of David"* and asked for mercy. This is more than asking if Jesus has a denarius to spare for a blind beggar.

Even asking for mercy is a bit over the top, though you could see that as no more than "Pity a blind beggar, mister?" But the *"Son of David"* title is very near the mark. That's like recognising Jesus as The One; that's like seeing him as the person we've been hoping and expecting all these years, sent from God to sort out all our troubles.

We hope for the Son of David – the one some people call the Messiah – and we expect God to send him soon. This is the one who will free Israel from Roman occupation and restore the glory days of King David. Well, that's what our teachers tell us; that's what we want God to do for us. But a blind beggar whom we all know and recognise from sitting by the road day in day out calling Jesus of Nazareth *"Son of David"*?

Firstly, it seems really unlikely that this Jesus could be what we expect of the Son of David. Though, come to think of it, he does seem to have done some astounding things, if the stories are anything to go by. And he's said some things that would make you sit up and take notice, though he's always made his points by telling stories. The trouble is, even though the Son of David is who we hope for and expect, if enough people call him that, someone in authority will notice and feel threatened and clamp down on these crowds that follow Jesus everywhere.

Secondly, how can it be that a blind beggar like Bartimaeus would recognise the Son of David, when the people with the sight and the education and the power and authority haven't seen it?

And the third thing is that we're all having a great day crowding round Jesus, wondering if he's going to do or say anything controversial or amazing or awesome, and Bartimaeus is trying to attract his attention and steal the limelight. We all feel sorry for him, but we don't really want him trying to join in. He'll just hold everything up, because he can't see where he's going and needs helping and warning about steps and uneven surfaces.

And then Jesus hears him and stops and comes over, and we have to bring Bartimaeus to him. Not that we have to do much. Bartimaeus jumps up, flings his cloak aside with coins rolling all over the road. And when he comes, Jesus doesn't tell him to be quiet about the 'Son of David' bit; he doesn't even give him a coin to keep him quiet. Jesus speaks to him almost as though he's been expecting him and welcomes the interruption. He asks a simple question, *"What do you want me to do for you?"*

I say a *simple* question, but as I think about it, I see that it has many layers of meaning and many possibilities for an answer.

I stop and wonder for a moment, what *does* Bartimaeus want Jesus to do for him? Does he want some money? Does he want to stop having to beg? Does he want to live differently?

Does he really think Jesus can do something that would mean he didn't have to beg and would have a completely transformed life? Does he *really* want that? Because if he thinks he does, this could be quite a challenging question.

I don't have long to ponder the possibilities in Jesus' question because Bartimaeus is answering immediately: *"Rabbi, I want to see."*[103]

That answers my doubts about Bartimaeus. He's either completely lost the plot or he's become so desperate that he'll ask any rumoured celebrity to do the impossible. Then a third possibility occurs to me, just as Jesus is speaking again. I suppose it's possible that Bartimaeus

---

[103] Mark 10:51 (MSG)

knows or believes something about Jesus of Nazareth that the rest of us haven't seen.

"Go," said Jesus, "your faith has healed you."[104]

And it's very clear that something has. I've never seen Bartimaeus – or anyone with even slight sight impairment – move the way he did. Instead of sitting at the back of the crowd and calling out to attract attention in the hope of receiving a small donation, Bartimaeus was at the front, walking along as near as he could get to Jesus, dodging round other people and trees, stepping over stones along the way. Bartimaeus showed every sign of wanting to stay with Jesus all day and probably go with him all the way to Jerusalem, if that's where he's going.

I must say that now I've seen Jesus perform a miracle of healing with my own eyes, I'm inclined to be with Bartimaeus and call him 'Son of David'. And if that's who he is, I'm sure he is going all the way to Jerusalem and I've no doubt that's what they'll call him there as well. The story of what he's done on the way into Jericho is already getting ahead of him. Others are coming out to try and see what's going on. I think I even glimpsed that greedy old tax collector Zacchaeus just now. The Jerusalem crowds will certainly have heard about this by the time Jesus gets there. What will happen then is certainly something to watch out for.[105]

---

[104] Mark 10:52 (TNIV)

[105] I don't often write in 'narrative style' and even less often do I preach that way. However, this struck me as a way to open up some of the surprises and some of the issues related to the account of the healing of Bartimaeus. It can be helpful to see an event through the eyes of someone who might have been amongst the crowd. In this way of telling, readers will notice that I use the verb 'to see' in the literal sense of noticing something and taking in information visually as well as the sense of 'to realise'. The one who can't 'see' has 'seen' a truth that sighted people haven't 'seen'. I have also taken the opportunity to point out the context of this episode. In Mark's account it is the last stage on the way to Jerusalem. I have tried to point out the links between Jesus' entry into Jericho and his entry into Jerusalem. I have also indicated that this is an episode also found in other Gospels. St. Luke's account of the healing of a blind beggar on the way into Jericho is followed by his encounter with Zacchaeus the tax collector, whose life was also transformed by his encounter with Jesus. The question is, what happens if you imagine yourself in the crowd? Or try to put yourself in the place of Bartimaeus?

20

Jesus on Terminal Illness

John 11:1-16

Now a certain man was ill, Lazarus of Bethany, the village of Mary and her sister Martha. Mary was the one who anointed the Lord with perfume and wiped his feet with her hair; her brother Lazarus was ill. So the sisters sent a message to Jesus, 'Lord, he whom you love is ill.' But when Jesus heard it, he said, 'This illness does not lead to death; rather it is for God's glory, so that the Son of God may be glorified through it.' Accordingly, though Jesus loved Martha and her sister and Lazarus, after having heard that Lazarus was ill, he stayed two days longer in the place where he was.

Then after this he said to the disciples, 'Let us go to Judea again.' The disciples said to him, 'Rabbi, the Jews were just now trying to stone you, and are you going there again?' Jesus answered, 'Are there not twelve hours of daylight? Those who walk during the day do not stumble, because they see the light of this world. But those who walk at night stumble, because the light is not in them.' After saying this, he told them, 'Our friend Lazarus has fallen asleep, but I am going there to awaken him.' The disciples said to him, 'Lord, if he has fallen asleep, he will be all right.' Jesus, however, had been speaking about his death, but they thought that he was referring merely to sleep. Then Jesus told them plainly, 'Lazarus is dead. For your sake I am glad I was not there, so that you may believe. But let us go to him.' Thomas, who was called the Twin, said to his fellow-disciples, 'Let us also go, that we may die with him.'

I wonder what your reaction is if you hear that a friend is unwell? There are many possibilities, but I suspect most of us instinctively want to be with them, to visit, to be in touch or to send a card. Heightened awareness of the dangers of infections might mean we tend towards 'being in touch' or 'sending a card'.

I suspect that our desire to go to someone we know who is ill would be even greater if we knew there was something we could do about it.

There are few things that friends can do medically that a trained medic can't, but if we knew our friend needed a kidney transplant and somehow we also knew that one of ours would be compatible, we would probably want to offer.

John goes to some lengths to let us know that Jesus cared very much for Lazarus and his sisters Martha and Mary. He had stayed at their house before, and he had commended Mary for her devotion and her desire to listen and learn. Martha and Mary's message to Jesus was that *"the one you love is ill"*[106]. John reiterates this by telling us that *"Jesus loved Martha and her sister and Lazarus"*[107].

The little words and the 'joining' words in accounts like this are often important. John 11:5 (just quoted) is followed by John 11:6, which begins, *"So..."* And we think, "So... he left what he was doing and rushed to be by his friend's side?" Or, "So... he sent a message immediately to say he would come as soon as he could?"

But no. *"So when he heard that Lazarus was ill, he stayed where he was two more days..."*[108]

My reaction to that is, "WHAT?!"

His friend is ill; he knows, more than anyone, he can do something for him; and he stays where he is?! OK, we know, because we've seen it in previous episodes, that Jesus can heal from a distance, so maybe that's what he's doing. Maybe we'll read that when he does get there, he'll be told that Lazarus recovered at the exact time he got the message about his illness.

The next verses explain why he might not have wanted to go to Lazarus even though he knew he could help. Two days later, when Jesus does suggest they go back to Judea,[109] his disciples are surprised

---

[106] John 11:3
[107] John 11:5
[108] John 11:6 (TNIV)
[109] John 11:7

because of their experiences there last time when the Jews tried to stone him.

Maybe Jesus has overcome his fear of being stoned? Or maybe he's decided that his friend's health is more important than his own safety?

We might want to step back a bit and say that surely, in the eternal scheme of things, his safety is paramount if he is to fulfil God's purposes for Israel and the world? Going back to Judea to be stoned for a religious argument in order to treat a sick friend, at the expense of the salvation of humanity, might be thought to be foolish in the extreme. This is not, however, what St Paul meant by being *"fools for Christ"*.

So, what does John mean by starting verse 6 with *"So..."*?

As we read on, it becomes apparent that either Jesus is getting secret updates on Lazarus's condition or he has some means of knowing what's going on and is seeing an opportunity for something much more significant than another healing.

By whatever means Jesus was keeping up with Lazarus's condition, he hasn't shared it with the disciples. They seem to be happy with that, but when they hear that Lazarus has fallen asleep, they assume this means that he's had a fever which has now passed its peak and he will recover if he sleeps. On the basis of this assumption, the disciples question Jesus' medical practice on the basis that sleep would be good for him so it wouldn't help to go and wake him up.

It seems Jesus can't get anything right at the moment. Not going to Lazarus straight away seemed an unnatural and unfriendly decision at the beginning; going to Lazarus to wake him up from a sleep that might do him good seems equally odd two days later.

But John explains that Jesus didn't mean that sort of sleep. We have the same issue here as with Jairus's daughter. In that instance, the people at Jairus's house knew that the girl was dead, and Jesus said that she was sleeping. Here Jesus knows that Lazarus is dead and still calls it sleep. It seems that Jesus cannot accept death. In his terms, an illness cannot be terminal.

It reminds us that when we read about death in the Bible, we need to be clear what definition of death is referred to. Is it about the biological workings of the body being disrupted to the extent that it cannot continue to breathe and move and pump blood round? Or is it about the person being separated from God? The distinction comes from right at the start of the Bible, where God tells Adam that if he eats from the tree of the knowledge of good and evil, he *"will certainly die"[110]*. The snake tells Eve that they *"will not certainly die"[111]*. They eat the fruit and they don't die, but they are separated from God by shame and pain and by exclusion from the Garden of Eden.[112]

The writings in the Bible are not designed to show that God might get something wrong. So we must conclude that what God means by death is different from what the snake meant and from what we have come to understand. The alternative at that point in the Bible is that when God said that Adam would die, he didn't mean immediately. The snake correctly pointed out that the fruit wasn't poisonous in the sense that it would kill them on the spot; however, he neglected to mention that God was right that death would then enter the equation and their lives would be limited.[113]

That sounds good to us who are used to one hundred years being exceptional, but if you have no concept of death at all, I suppose 930 is a bit limited. On this basis, and from all human experience, life is a terminal illness. We're told that there's nothing in life so certain as death (and taxes). But Jesus, especially in John's Gospel, seems not to agree. He talks about eternal life and doesn't seem to believe in terminal illness.

If we don't have these two different understandings of death, Jesus is being confusing when talking with his disciples about Lazarus. When he first hears that Lazarus is ill he tells them that *"this illness will not end in death"[114]*. That seems to be borne out by the news that Lazarus has fallen asleep and will therefore get better.[115] But then Jesus tells them plainly, *"Lazarus is dead."[116]*

I can almost hear the disciples saying, "But you said this illness wouldn't end in death!"

And that is exactly the point. Lazarus died but that's not the end of the story for Lazarus. Naturally we stray from 'Jesus on terminal

[110] Genesis 2:17
[111] Genesis 3:4
[112] Genesis 3:6-24
[113] Genesis 5:5
[114] John 11:4
[115] John 11:12
[116] John 11:14

illness' to 'Jesus on death'. As we know, if we've read the rest of the chapter, Jesus raises Lazarus from the dead. Like the other miracles that John tells us about, this is a sign which points us to a truth that John wants us to note.

The raising of Lazarus combined with Jesus' statement to Martha that *"I am the Resurrection and the Life"*[117] is about there being more to life than life. This first part of the account, up to the point where we hear plainly that Lazarus is dead, makes the same point: life doesn't end with death.

Later, both Martha and Mary say to Jesus, *"If you had been here my brother would not have died."*[118] In one sense it indicates that they may not have heard about times when Jesus healed from a distance. In another sense it demonstrates that death has no power in Jesus' presence. In his eternal scheme of things, there is no such thing as terminal illness – not even life itself is terminal.

Jesus told his disciples that they would go to Lazarus *"so that you may believe"*[119]. We must conclude that they would believe, as Martha and Mary would believe, and as we will also come to believe from this sign, that through Jesus and through trust in him, eternal life in God's presence is what it's all about on both sides of the grave.

---

[117] John 11:25
[118] John 11:21,32
[119] John 11:15

Also by David Muskett

Jesus on Gardening
ISBN 978-1-911086-28-4

When Jesus taught, he often used stories that his listeners would be able to relate to – each one revealing something about God's activity on Earth. David Muskett looks at what Jesus said about horticulture and agriculture – and finds parallels in our British love for gardening. These short, easily digestible sermons will leave you inspired and empowered to see God's Kingdom grow in your own local neighbourhood.

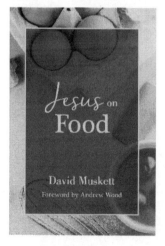

Jesus on Food
ISBN 978-1-78815-698-1

When Jesus spoke to his disciples, he often used everyday experiences to teach them valuable spiritual lessons. Here David Muskett looks at the many times when Jesus used food and mealtimes to reveal principles of God's Kingdom, finding parallels in our British love of baking and fine dining. These short, easily digestible sermons will leave you inspired and empowered to live out your everyday life from an eternal, heavenly perspective.

Available from your local bookshop or from the publisher:

www.onwardsandupwards.org/shop